Clo
The Clowns of Technology:

Clones:
The Clowns of Technology?

D. Gareth Jones

paternoster
press

Paternoster Press is an imprint of Paternoster Publishing,
P.O. Box 300, Carlisle, Cumbria, CA3 0QS, UK
and
P.O. Box 1047, Waynesboro, GA 30830-2047, USA
Website: www.paternoster-publishing.com

British Library Cataloguing in Publication Data

A catalogue record for this book is available from the British Library

ISBN 1-84227-086-9

Cover Design by Campsie, Glasgow
Typeset by WestKey Ltd, Falmouth, Cornwall
Printed in Great Britain by Omnia Books Ltd, Glasgow

Contents

Preface

Why write yet another book on cloning? There have been numerous ones over the past four or so years, and it is more than likely that the flood of books on this intriguing topic will continue unabated. Is this book nothing more than a part of the flood? It may be, but I hope not. The reason for this is that I see cloning as something much larger than the technique of nuclear replacement. Of course, it is this, but it is also part of a far bigger venture, fitting as it does into the whole area that has become the artificial reproductive technologies. As we contemplate what cloning is and what prospects it opens up for us, we come face to face with what we want from biomedical technology.

For some people a statement like this is akin to the kiss of death for cloning. While artificial reproductive technologies, even *in vitro* fertilization in its simplest form, are bad enough, a far more extreme technique like cloning is the harbinger of disaster. Humanity is in danger of self-destructing as we aim to change what makes us human and to improve on what nature has given us. It is no wonder that the shutters have gone up since cloning made the headlines in 1997.

The trouble is that since Dolly the sheep came on the scene, cloning has been equated with human reproductive cloning. Everywhere we look we see pictures of identical babies, identical tyrants, and identical heroes, as though this is what human cloning will amount to. The hysteria and misinformation behind these depictions are hard to comprehend. Surely people are aware of the subtleties and promise of cloning? Surely they know that we could not produce all these identical people even if we wanted to? Surely they realize that scientists do not spend their time in acts of meaningless bravado? I'm not sure. All one can say is that this duplication motif has dominated discussions, so much so that presidents, prime ministers, government committees, and parliaments have been swept away by a tide of fear and resentment. One of my aims in this book is to try to place cloning in a more realistic setting.

This is not some theoretical exercise, aimed at those who like intellectual conundrums or who are fascinated by scientific wizardry at the beginning of human life – cloning is far too serious an issue to waste time in such a manner. I want to face my readers with real challenges, so that we might begin to dig deep into cloning: to discover what it is all about and to look at the world into which this technology is rapidly taking us. I have no intention, however, of coming up with standard answers or of telling my readers what they should think. Instead, I intend to work issues through, and perhaps some of my conclusions will come as a surprise, even an unwelcome surprise.

I am writing from the viewpoint of a biologist, with a Christian perspective. My approach is informed by my training and interests as a scientist, and especially as an anatomist with specific interests in early human development and in neurobiology. I am deeply committed to the scientific approach, which I view as complementing my Christian approach, rather than being in opposition to it. This undoubtedly makes me more open than many to accepting scientific innovations, even at the beginning of human life. I make no apology for this, since I shall attempt to justify every position I adopt.

For me, cloning is a parable. It will tell us a great deal about how we live our lives, about our expectations and aspirations and about our world-view. If Jesus were on earth today, he might well have used it as one of his parables. The question is, what would he have said? I shall aim to work out what might have been the ingredients of his parable, and I may of course be wrong, but I hope my reasoning will be provocative and helpful.

Some of the material here has been tried out on groups to

whom I have spoken, including my home church – Dunedin City Baptist Church – meetings of the International Christian Medical and Dental Association, the Royal Society of Edinburgh, and the International Association of Bioethics. I would like to thank those associated with these organizations for giving me the opportunity to develop my thinking, often in controversial ways.

The first time I wrote about cloning was in my book *Brave New People*, published in 1984. At that time what I wrote was largely ignored, even though some of the other chapters in the book were intensely scrutinized – as so often happens, little interest is shown in topics that have not as yet become newsworthy. Subsequent to that I paid little attention to the subject even though I wrote a great deal about a large range of issues at the initial stages of human life. I, like others, thought cloning was an unlikely possibility, and was not worthy of being explored in any serious ethical writings. How wrong I was!

This book is the latest in a series on biomedical issues written from a Christian perspective, *Brave New People*, *Manufacturing Humans*, and *Valuing People*, all of which provide the backdrop to the current book. While each of the previous books has touched on highly newsworthy and contemporary issues, this one fits even more obviously into this genre.

I have written this book alongside the myriad administrative commitments involved in running a large university department, and in between a host of lectures on the nervous system. Most of it has been done in snatches of time, generally in the evenings, at home, in airports and on long flights between countries. I trust the end result is not as fragmented as this might suggest.

I would like to thank Kerry Galvin for carrying out library searches, for thoroughly checking every draft of every chapter, and for improving it in many small ways. Above all, I would like to acknowledge the support of Beryl, my wife, for quietly putting up with my constant writing and thinking. She is always in the background as one talk after another, one article after another, and even one book after another, gets in the way of normal civilized behaviour on my part.

Gareth Jones

One

A Parable For Our Century

The term 'clone' or 'cloning' is used very widely in everyday speech. Only the other day, when talking in my university about the relationship between supervisors and postgraduate students, I referred to 'academic supervisory cloning'. Of course, I had no intention of suggesting that supervisors set out to clone their students biologically; what I had in mind was that supervisors may sometimes attempt to so train their students that the latter end up just like their supervisors.

We repeatedly use this form of speech, because we all know what we mean by it. To clone someone is to make them like the person who gave rise to them (my clone is like me), and while this may be used in a fairly neutral way, very often it is used negatively. There is an element of restricting the freedom of clones to be themselves – I want to coerce them to be like me rather than allow them to become themselves. It is hardly surprising, then, that when we talk about actual biological cloning our tendency is to think about cloning in the same way. This is why there has been such a huge emphasis on human reproductive cloning; producing people to order, to be exactly like existing people, to coerce them to follow in these other people's footsteps, to be xeroxed, to be mass-produced.

This is fine, but we need to go a little further in unpacking this term. 'Clone' is a term that comes from the Greek word, *klōn*, meaning 'twig', 'slip' or 'cutting'. One dictionary entry describes it as 'a group of organisms formed asexually from one ancestor'. Cloning refers to reproduction by asexual means, with the result that the new individual or individuals are derived from a single parent and are genetically identical to that parent. It is the production of a cell or organism with the same nuclear genome as another cell or organism.

In order to produce a 'clone' of an organism that normally reproduces sexually, the nucleus of a mature unfertilized egg has to be removed and replaced with a nucleus having the full complement of chromosomes. This latter nucleus may be from a specialized body cell of an adult organism (a somatic cell), or from an embryo or fetus. If this process is repeated with the transferred nucleus coming from the same source as in the first instance, the result is an unlimited number, or clone of identical individuals. These second-generation individuals are all identical to the original individual from which they were derived. The word 'clone' is treated like the word 'sheep', in that it is used to refer to both singular and plural entities, at the same time maintaining the idea that a clone is an offspring with an identical genetic constitution to its single parent.

The dominant picture of cloning used by the media is that of the xeroxing of human beings. It is depicted as a means of obtaining 1, 20, 100 or 1,000 copies of a human being, all genetically the same as the person from whom they were produced. Theoretically, this process confers a form of genetic immortality on the original person, particularly if second-generation clones are subsequently made from first-generation clones, and so on, throughout the generations. The power of this picture cannot be underestimated, since virtually every popular article about cloning has a series of identical photos of a delightful infant, popular hero, or political tyrant. All such representations of human cloning are as misleading and mischievous as they are provocative. Nevertheless, cloning as a science fiction genre has dominated the human imagination for a very long time.

Cloning is seen by some as a metaphor and a mirror, allowing us to look at ourselves and our values, and so decide what is important to us and why. It also reflects the place of science in our world. Is science a threat or a promise, and are scientists sages or villains?

For many commentators, the answer to this question is self-evident. Cloning has become a metaphor for unbridled science. Since the 1970s, biological science has been viewed with scepticism by the public at large; it has taken on a fearful facade, with scientists being viewed as intrinsically untrustworthy. Gina Kolata, in her book *Clone: The Road to Dolly, and the Path Ahead*, has described this transition well, with scientists being increasingly viewed as beings driven by curiosity, and more by a perverse glee in manipulating life than by moral qualms about what is proper and appropriate. It is this enduring distrust of science and scientists that has made cloning a subject of notoriety and poor taste. All sections of society, including the Christian community, are affected.

The cloning of a human being has become a symbol of the unforgivable scientific sin. Hence, serious discussion of cloning – any form of cloning – is mired in this symbol of laboratory maleficence. The public has been alerted to this Faustian bargain, and it will not lightly forget the price science is exacting for its ill-gotten gains. Cloning has become a metaphor for the temptation of scientists to play God, a metaphor which however misused and twisted has extraordinary power to frighten and appal. The bravado of fearless scientists is detested and condemned. It seems that cloning is viewed by many as the epitome of biologists' knowing sin, just as physicists had known sin with the development of the atom bomb. People even talk about genetic bomb shelters. The problem with this analogy is that cloning is not a weapon of aggression, even if it were to be used in ways of which many would disapprove.

Far away from these dire prognostications, and returning to the laboratory, there is a high likelihood that in future years cloning may become one of the most sophisticated of all the artificial reproductive technologies. This is not because numerous human individuals will be produced by cloning, but because it will be used for therapeutic purposes and as a means of assisting infertile couples to have children of their own. This is a far more subtle form of cloning than generally imagined, where the intentions are good and humanitarian, and without the startling

bravado so often associated with the cloning of humans. This is
not the nightmare vision of hundreds of identical people wander-
ing around like robots, but of human embryonic material being
put to powerful therapeutic uses, and of children being produced
by cloning for loving parents with the best of intentions.
Children truly are 'made' with this technique; this is its biological
potential and its moral uncertainty. This may be inevitable with
any technique that so emphasizes the manufacturing side of
reproduction, but it does not automatically make it
unacceptable.

It will become evident later on in this book that the cloning of
complete individuals (what I shall refer to as *human reproductive cloning*) is not what I think is important about cloning; in
fact, I think it is a distraction. However, I have to start at this
point, and I shall discuss a number of aspects of human reproductive cloning in the first few chapters. In order to do this I shall
embark on a thought process, glancing into the future at a society
where cloning has been accepted. This is a hypothetical society; it
exists only in my imagination, and yet it will help us explore
some of the ramifications of cloning. Through this hypothetical
society we shall explore the implications for us living as we do
in more 'primitive' societies, perhaps on the road to this more
'advanced' one.

Let us turn then to a report from this society of the future,
from 2060 to be exact.

Living with clones: an imaginary society of the future

In this society cloning is generally accepted. Animal cloning has
had considerable effects on agriculture, and many products used
in medical treatment are now manufactured via cloning in
animals. Cystic fibrosis sufferers are able to minimize damage to
their lungs and pancreas by the availability of a substance produced in large quantities in sheep's milk. A great deal has been
discussed about the mechanisms that switch genes on and off
during development, and huge strides have been made in

providing important insights into repair mechanisms in the brain and spinal cord, and also into the way in which cancerous cells revert to the embryonic stage and start multiplying uncontrollably. The result has been that neurological diseases like Parkinson's disease can be largely cured, and even Alzheimer's disease can often be controlled. Young people who were paralyzed by serious injury to their spinal cords can walk again. Most people are delighted by what cloning has achieved in these medical areas, this form of cloning often being referred to as *human therapeutic cloning*.

However, our imaginary society also has examples of human reproductive cloning, and it is on this that I want to concentrate. Of every thousand babies born in this society, twenty will have been cloned. Cloning, therefore, has made a major impact on this imaginary society. As we look at human reproductive cloning, I shall subdivide it into two categories: *ego cloning* and *medically justified reproductive cloning*. The techniques are identical, but the motives and aspirations of the two seem to be very different.

Ego cloning

Ego cloning is controlled by legislation, according to which one person is allowed a maximum of three clones, in order to restrict the extent of genetic conformity. There is an unexpected problem, though, and this is that clones are turning out to be far more variable than anticipated. Quite apart from the age difference, they are not nearly as similar in personality as are identical twins. In some cases, it is hard to recognize that the individuals are clones at all. Not only this, some clones have been positively disappointing.

Individuals are frustrated when 'my' clone has my failings, as well as my strengths. This should have been obvious to everyone, but perhaps those who want to have themselves cloned overlook the very simple fact that they actually have failings. People who have had themselves cloned have been surprised when the clone has turned out to have totally different interests from themselves (the new 'me' is more unlike 'me' than I had thought possible). This is proving especially difficult when the clone of the self-made businessman-cum-philanthropist turns out to be a budding philosopher uninterested in money and abysmal at making any!

Ego cloning has proved something of a failure, especially in those families where the clones have been treated as slaves – created to do their masters' will. This was what the horror stories suggested would happen, and in some instances it has. The problem here is that clones have been treated as less than human. In other words, major problems arise when clones are forced to behave as others expect them to behave. This is the crux of the issue. Why accept someone so different from you, when you brought them into the world to be like you?

Ego cloning is the sort of cloning I shall dismiss as unworthy of serious reflection. I hope that my imaginary world has shown why this is the case. In some respects ego cloning will probably not be as bad as most people anticipate, but on the other hand, it probably will not achieve much either. Once clones are given freedom to be individuals, and are allowed to develop as themselves, ego cloning becomes redundant; it is something of a farce, an all-too-obvious example of a tragic technical excess.

The most widely expressed fear is that the resulting clones would be psychologically harmed, with a diminished sense of individuality and personal autonomy. This is a pragmatic argument, which may or may not turn out to be valid. It requires critical assessment, since even human clones will be exposed to different environments, different cultural pressures in different generations, and therefore vastly different experiences. In practice, they will be far less like one another than are natural identical twins, who generally demonstrate as much individuality as anyone else. In other words, a dissimilar genetic identity is not essential for human beings to feel, and indeed be, individuals in their own right.

Basic to how human clones are regarded are the motives for bringing them into existence. If they are produced 'to order', their value in the eyes of their progenitors would appear to lie in the extent to which they replicate a previous person or are able to carry out certain predetermined tasks. The danger here is that they would not be valued as unique individuals, but would simply be judged in terms of their ability to perform specified functions or demonstrate specified traits. In so far as cloning is used to treat human beings as solely of functional value to society or to groups within society, it would undermine the intrinsic worth and dignity of human beings. This is to be avoided at all costs, but is it inevitable?

The 'most successful' ego cloning from the viewpoint of the progenitors of the clones will be those who are denied the freedom to be themselves. But this can only be accomplished by treating them as sub-human, as having less value than other people. This is the ultimate condemnation of ego cloning, as it is of all forms of repression. But one does not need the technical expertise of cloning to treat others in repressive ways.

This form of cloning is the closest we come to producing children 'to order'. What is reprehensible here is the drive to propagate my features for my alleged benefit, paying little thought to the interests and concerns of the resulting child. There is no justification that I can find for using technology for this end, and I have every sympathy with those who condemn cloning in this guise.

But this is only one form of human reproductive cloning. There is another, in which the driving force is quite different, even though the technology is identical.

Medically justified reproductive cloning

In our imaginary society, a couple in which one partner has a genetic defect can avoid the risk of passing on this defect to their children by having cloned children of the healthy partner. In other couples, where the male partner is unable to produce gametes, cloning of the woman is a means of bypassing his sterility. It is at this point that cloning resembles more conventional practices, ranging from adoption, to artificial insemination by donor (DI), and to techniques such as intracytoplasmic sperm injection (ICSI).

However, cloning has also been widely used outside a marital relationship, to enable single women, or lesbian couples to have children. Some gay men and the occasional single man, have also used it, but they have had to employ women as surrogates. The practice has been difficult to control, because once a technique is available the drive to use it everywhere imaginable is very strong. Cloning has also become divorced from any moral values. Its nature appears to be such that it is simply used as a means of enabling anyone at all to have children outside any conventional commitment relationship. Controls appear ineffective, stemming possibly from the technique itself, with its almost complete emphasis on the manufacturing side of reproduction.

Some people have cloned one of their children so that the clone could be the compatible bone marrow donor for a much needed bone marrow transplantation. This has its problems, but the clone's life is not placed at risk, and in reality this differs little from those who years ago had another child (naturally) for the same reason. In fact one is assured of a compatible donor, something that is not the case if one has another child by natural reproductive means. In most such cases, the resulting child or clone is loved and cared for as an individual in his or her own right.

As we contemplate these possibilities, we have to admit that cloning may prove beneficial for infertile couples. It will prove hard to condemn the couples who one day use it in these instances, and the resulting clones (children) will probably be as well adjusted as are any other children. This is because they will be brought into existence to be themselves; the fact that they will be genetically identical to their mothers will not be the reason for resorting to cloning. They would be created to be loved and to love. Just as the first IVF (*in vitro* fertilization) children turned out to be far more normal and unexceptional than some had supposed, the same will probably be true of these cloned children. The similarities with existing artificial reproductive technologies will undoubtedly be considerable.

As with IVF, one needs to ask what is the real cost of producing these children, not for the individuals concerned, but for society? The cost appears to be in the price society may be paying for having accepted cloning into its midst. This is not the horror some imagine; it is far more subtle than that. It is in changed societal expectations of children, and of the manner in which they can be produced. I do not consider that this inevitably condemns cloning, but it does place cloning for reasons of infertility into a much broader, and more encompassing, context.

What about the cloning of a dying child? Such an act would encourage parents to produce one child in the image of another, and yet the parents would not be 'getting back' the same child as the one who had been lost. Cloning under these circumstances may encourage society to view children as interchangeable commodities, but is this substantially different from what already happens when a couple has a child by natural means shortly after the death of another child in infancy?

The question raised by such possibilities is whether we are ever justified in producing 'another me'. This is not ego cloning, because it is not my goal and longing to produce 'another me'. In medically justified reproductive cloning, it is serious medical treatment, just as the assisted reproductive technologies are serious medical treatment. But how easy will it be to live with 'another me', when that person into whose eyes I look is not actually me? The argument will be, of course, that I did not want that person to be another me; I wanted another person – a child – and not a replica of myself. Even the most naturally fertilized of my children has something of me in them, and I cannot ignore that something – for good or ill.

In the light of these considerations, it may be preferable to have no children rather than a cloned child, but it has to be admitted that neither way is easy. It also has to be remembered that many people have had to resort to unpalatable measures to overcome infertility – DI, IVF, ICSI or adoption. Should they have chosen childlessness instead? Cloning can now be added to this ever-lengthening and increasingly ambiguous list of unclear possibilities.

A society that accepts cloning in a few circumscribed situations finds it almost impossible to limit its use to just those situations. Perhaps all technologies are the same. Does cloning represent a new dimension or merely an extension to what we already accept or tolerate? Is it pushing the boundaries too far, or are we simply afraid of the unknown? These are difficult questions for everyone, Christians included. I am not attempting to diminish the difficulties, but neither do I think we can by-pass them by pretending that cloning is so horrendous that it does not bear serious reflection. We have to take it seriously, and we have to face up to what may appear to be unpalatable possibilities. But if they are unpalatable, we must have cogent reasons for knowing why this is the case.

Human clones as research tools

Let us return to our imaginary society, and enquire what was done about using human clones (those who have been born and have lives of their own) as research tools. This is the closest we come to science fiction scenarios – Aldous Huxley's depictions in *Brave New World* were almost correct. Is it possible to do research on human clones in an ethical manner, if the clones themselves can have no say in what is done to them? What this amounts to is producing human beings (clones) in order to sacrifice them when organs or tissues are required.

Identical twins have been around throughout recorded history, and few societies have allowed one to be sacrificed in order to save the life of the other (the agonies experienced when Siamese twins have to be separated demonstrates this). If we do not do this with identical twins, why do it with human clones? To do it with humans would take us back to the dark days of human experimentation, rather than into some glorious future. The people of our imaginary society also thought this way.

The result is that there have been no moves to produce research clones. Experiments on animal clones have been extensively used, but not on human clones. Although considerable pressures have been exerted by a few scientists to go in this direction, as a society we have concluded that the drawbacks are too great.

A clear moral line has been set, and there is no longer serious discussion about research clones. To destroy human clones so that others might live is considered outlandish even by those who normally think little about ethical matters. Such gross devaluation of human beings is not tolerated. Once clones have been born, they are to be treated in the same manner as any other human being.

Over against this extreme form of experimentation, there is the far more scientifically challenging task of using very early embryos (four-, eight- or sixteen-cell stage) to serve as a source of human tissues and possibly organs. This is human therapeutic cloning and not human reproductive cloning, and it has been widely accepted in our imaginary society, where research laboratories are licensed to carry out research using early human embryos.

The competing forces in this instance are the dignity of such early human embryos and the dignity of those who may benefit from the tissues that one day will be produced from such embryonic tissue. The question with which we have to grapple is whether we can truly speak about dignity on the two sides of this argument. Do such four-, eight- or sixteen-cell embryos have dignity? Do they have a dignity bestowed upon them by God? On the other hand, if we talk about the dignity of those who may benefit from this particular form of treatment, what are the consequences of this when the technology is available but we refuse to develop it? And where does God come into this? I shall return to these issues in later chapters.

Will Christians accept cloning?

Back in our imaginary society in 2060, something totally unexpected occurred.

> A fascinating situation has arisen in a number of churches. A surprisingly large number of Christian groups have gone in for medically justified reproductive cloning. Even those Christians and Christian groups who were implacably opposed to cloning of any description a few years ago are now prepared to accept that it may sometimes have a part to play in the lives of Christian couples. There is still enormous discussion about this, and some churches have disciplined their members for doing so. However, this is very uncommon. For most it is now a part of the medical armamentarium in difficult reproductive areas. Needless to say, the resulting children are deeply loved, and outsiders have no idea that cloning has been involved in bringing them into the world.

I am deliberately being mischievous and provocative here, by suggesting that many Christians who currently are strongly opposed to cloning will change their minds once cloning becomes a reality. You may not agree with such a cynical perspective. However, this has happened repeatedly in the past, and I see no reason why it will not happen again in the future. Whenever this happens, it is because the original opposition to a new procedure or technique has not been based on a solid foundation, either in science or theology; and this may apply to some forms of cloning.

But I could go even further. Consider the following even more unlikely scenario from this future society.

> Some Christian groups have gone in for reproductive cloning, because they wanted to clone the good preachers in their midst (the expositors actually). Who could blame them when decent expositors are in short supply? Some seemed to work well, and a few leading preachers are indeed clones. This

reminds me of the old days when sons took on the mantle of their fathers, even though they generally never had quite the abilities or gifts of the fathers. But, again like the old days, some clones have been ghastly mistakes. They aren't even Christians, let alone great expositors of the word. The mistake these people have made is to think that God is limited by genetics.

Unlikely as this scenario may be, it reminds us of some basic principles: just because there is genetic similarity between two individuals does not ensure there will be spiritual similarity. The cloners forgot that God does not work like this, otherwise faith would run in families and there would be no hope for anyone not born into a Christian family. Cloned creations have their own responsibility to respond to the overtures of God, and they may not do this in spite of being cloned replicas of their faithful fathers or mothers. There are no such people as cloned Christians; faith cannot be cloned. By the same token, evil cannot be cloned either. Even clones reared in Christian families may walk away from faith.

It is all too easy to fail to appreciate fully the uniqueness and individuality of each person. We are tempted to mould likeness and conformity into people; we may be tempted to have churches full of similar people, believing the same things, having the same attitudes, and acting in the same ways. This is not what responding to the overtures of God is all about, whether in a non-cloning or in a cloning society. God deals with each one separately because he views all as distinct individuals.

If cloned individuals ever do exist, they will be far more human than frequently imagined. They will stand before God as ordinary human individuals, and will be just as responsible for their actions and motives as anyone else. They will be able to respond to God and have a personal relationship with him through Christ, in exactly the same way as their non-cloned counterparts.

Nevertheless, the cloning of humans should not be pursued without enormous reservations. Even when clones turn out well as human beings, we should be left with a nagging doubt, because the individuality and unpredictability of human life may have been diminished. This is sometimes expressed by stating that cloning is a tool and a means to an end, and that humans will be made to order like toys in a factory. There is undoubtedly an element of this in cloning – even for infertility – and yet the extent of the 'to order' scenario would be far less than frequently imagined. Cloning does not enable us to manipulate and change a person's characteristics at will, or to construct a person to specifications. To suggest otherwise, is to claim for cloning far greater power than it will have. Beyond this, whatever a person's characteristics and however acquired, God will still deal with him or her as he does with ordinary people, and that is as a unique individual. This is God's grace, cloning or no cloning.

It is all very well thinking about cloning in terms of producing identical people, but what might that mean when expressed within a Christian context? Down through the centuries people have used numerous means of attempting to make others profess the Christian faith. Some of these have been well meaning but misguided, others have been perverse. Surely, we should have learned that true conversion is a work of God, and not a result of either psychological or genetic manipulation.

Clones as people

Our imaginary society in 2060 brings home to us our ability to conform to, and live with, the secular response to technological and medical developments. It teaches us that Christians have a role to play and that role is not a clear-cut, black-and-white one. We have to sift through the mire of doomsday predictions and narcissistic expectations and emerge with a position that is faithful to biblical teaching and that will glorify God. We may not agree with the direction society has taken, yet we have to continue to be part of that society, to be a light for that society and to play a prophetic role.

The temptation to close our eyes, and run away from hard decision making has to be resisted. Human clones will be people

– to be valued as anyone else is valued. No matter what procedures may be used to bring clones into existence, once in existence they are people created by God, with a God-bestowed dignity, with the gift of human life, and with the prospects and expectations of anyone round about them. Clones will be far more like the rest of us than they are like the science fiction depiction of human-like robots.

Cloning is an extreme technique. As such, it is to be analysed even more rigorously than are other technological procedures in the reproductive area. However, it fits at one end of a well-known continuum that extends all the way to contraception at the other end. Like all other technological procedures, it confronts us with human responsibility and irresponsibility, with human wisdom and foolishness, and with the ever-present message that we are to look to God for guidance and direction. The danger in the end is that human beings think they are omnipotent and all wise, able to do anything. Clones remind us that this is a dangerous and foolhardy illusion.

Cloning needs to be seen against the role of technology in human life and human society, especially against the background of what constitutes modern medicine. The extent to which we depend both upon God's grace and human ingenuity will come to the fore. The challenge here is to depend upon God, regardless of the extent of any technology and of human achievements.

Ultimately, we have to come face to face with the new biotechnology. If Christians fail to do this, in order to attack philosophical and theological straw men so that they can return to some pre-technology theology, they will have failed in their duty as the Lord's people to transform contemporary culture. It is crucial that we take seriously the extent of biological control that is on our doorstep.

Were human cloning to become reality, it would soon emerge that it is a two-edged sword; the pressures it would unleash would be similar to those unleashed by all the other technologies used to control and manipulate human reproduction. Society has been changed for ever by them, and Christian standards have been placed under enormous pressure. Technologies like these have to be harnessed for good ends, but different agendas within society make this exceedingly difficult, if not impossible. Life may well be easier if cloning never eventuates in humans, but that does not set cloning apart. What we have in cloning is a cautionary tale about all scientific ventures into the reproductive unknown.

Why not clowns instead?

Clones have a fascination for many people, encompassing our love for technology and our longing to exert ever-increasing control over our environment and our progeny. But they may prove to be the clowns of technology. What might this mean, and what are clowns?

The first point to note about clowns is their dress and antics, which reinforce our view of them as lowly, insignificant figures, surrounded by forces beyond their control but never beyond their ability to provoke laughter. Their inconsequential bumblings are caricatures of our own folly; they reveal what we seek to hide, and yet these revelations are manifestations of one aspect of the human condition. They help us laugh at our failings, and in laughing to realize that humans are sometimes stupid and often frail. It is not surprising, therefore, that clowns are melancholy beings, underlining the irrational and uncontrolled in human existence.

Unlikely as it may sound, the clown enshrines one of the most fundamental of human attributes. This is the ability to ponder and meditate, and to indulge in activities that have no immediate goal. Humans are capable of play long after childhood has passed. One facet of this is the potential for self-criticism, and for laughing at oneself. To be human includes the ability to indulge in inconsequential humour and wit.

Clowning allows people to act in an eccentric way and, in so doing, to demonstrate to others the value of eccentricity. It is nothing less than an exploration of one's humanity. To deny a place for humour in life is to deny to people the potential to assess themselves as human beings.

Humour ensures that we, as humans, see ourselves in perspective. It shields us from making idols of ourselves or others, enabling us to acknowledge the limitations and discrepancies of human life. But humour in the incongruities of human existence is made possible only against the backdrop of a belief in the congruity and orderliness of human existence. In this it is at odds with sarcasm and cynicism, which question the meaning and value of human life.

It is significant that much of science fiction is grim, especially where humans have assumed responsibility for controlling other humans. There is no room for clowning, since life has become a harsh routine in which an elite controls and directs a subjugated populace. Inconsequential wit has no part to play in a world of robotic slaves; it has become superfluous and is readily dispensed with. In these futuristic visions the concept of human dignity has been lost. On the other hand, in situations where there is a high regard for the dignity of individuals, they are valued for who they are, regardless of their place in society. This is an essentially Christian stance, based on the reliability and steadfastness of the world, and of the intrinsic value of human beings. It is only in a world like this that individuals can be valued for themselves, and their eccentricities, oddities and incongruities can be accepted. When they are accepted as people whose value stems from what they are as ordinary beings, their potential for clowning and for expressing some of the absurdity and joy of human existence can emerge.

'To be oneself' is a fundamental prerequisite for human life. This may involve being different from others, going one's own way, refusing to conform to society's mores. While certain strictures are essential in any society, there must also be a requisite degree of freedom and self-expression. Once these are lost, so too is hope. And when hope is lost, only absurdity remains.

Clowns and clones (I am thinking of ego cloning here) respectively epitomize individuality and lack of individuality, diversity and conformity, creativity and compliance. Clowning allows for eccentricity and humour; it is in many respects a comic possibility; it acknowledges us to be what we are, no matter how grotesque; it gives us names, so that we can live out our individuality. Cloning (ego cloning), by contrast, demands predictability; it is pretentious, and sees us as little more than computerized units; it allows us to be only what we have been designed to be. The contrast between the two is similar to that between a cathedral with its gargoyles and many delightful nuances and a downtown skyscraper with its sterile functionality.

We should value clowns with their ability to make us assess ourselves and our goals, with their talent for forcing us to laugh at our pretensions and arrogance, and with their childlike guile that helps us see ourselves in perspective. We are not such impeccable geniuses that we have earned the right to manufacture future generations in our own image, whether by cloning or political conformity.

Should we even take seriously these grand designs or should we laugh at their arrogance? After all, biological cloning, even when a practical proposition in humans, will fail in its main intent; it will not produce individuals identical to the original people. Why bother? Why take our grand visions so seriously, knowing their tragic outcome? Why not sit back and question the purpose of such futility? Why not ponder a while and laugh at the incongruity of our efforts?

The way of the clown is not an easy one in a world dominated by scientific gadgetry and impersonal expertise. Nevertheless, it is a way we cannot afford to ignore, because it places human values above human technology so that human beings remain in control of the tools at their disposal. It is a means of ensuring that human beings are the measure of things, rather than man-made things determining the lines along which humans are themselves structured.

This is a challenge faced by all of us. Ours is a world of many forms of engineering, all of which are modifying human existence in quite dramatic ways. Such trends demand decisions about how we use these powers, decisions which depend upon fundamental attitudes and beliefs. Whether we want a race of clones is up to us, and whether we acquire such a race will depend upon whether we still believe in the virtues of clowning.

Coping with biomedical technology

Although we are still very much at the beginning of our journey, a number of points are emerging. General as these are at this stage, they will have repercussions for the manner in which we tackle far more detailed issues later on. These points can be articulated as follows.

We should not ignore the prospects and challenges of biomedical technology

Even if the world of 2060 as painted here may repel us, it is probably not as bad as some of the situations that have existed in one country after another over the past few years. While this does not justify human reproductive cloning, it reminds us that it should be seen in perspective. Societies are thrown into chaos by more than sophisticated technology. Some of the most brutish means of treating human beings have been technologically crude. If human reproductive cloning ever becomes reality, it will downgrade human value and human dignity to the extent that human clones are treated in degrading ways. If the latter does not eventuate, even this extreme form of cloning may be less worrying than most people currently think.

These reflections are not meant to justify human reproductive cloning; they simply remind us that our motives and intentions are paramount for ethical behaviour. Banning human reproductive cloning will not ensure that we act honourably towards one another; neither will it prevent scientific research on various forms of cloning from taking place in laboratories throughout the world. This is because the drive to understand basic developmental mechanisms in humans is too great, as is the allure of devising therapeutic strategies to cope with the major medical diseases of people in the twenty-first century.

Biomedical technology needs to be understood

The driving forces behind biomedical technology include the desire to control biological processes, both in health and disease. In principle, such a desire is to be welcomed. On the other hand, all technological approaches have their built-in limitations and shortcomings; in short, technology is not everything. To expect it to solve all our problems is itself one of our greatest failings.

As we acknowledge the limitations of technology, we need to acknowledge our own limitations. Our flawed understanding and lack of wisdom frequently let us down, failings that have major consequences as the technology at our disposal becomes increasingly powerful. This will be supremely demonstrated when, and if, we have the ability to clone other humans. While the power in our hands will be more apparent than real (we will still not be creators in any fundamental sense), symbolically we will have moved on to a completely new plane. We will feel that we are the makers and masters of others as never before. This will be an illusion, although as we shall see in a later chapter, human therapeutic cloning will bring us far closer to this intimidating position.

Nevertheless, we exert less control over technology than we think. It will never provide us with a perfect body or brain, partly because the technology at our disposal is incapable of such feats, and partly because we make mistakes. We are not up to such feats, and yet some writers refuse to accept this. A mixture of bravado and technical incompetence is dangerous; it will both mislead us and let us down. What is fascinating about discussions of human cloning is that most people seem to be aware of this in this particular area. They reject bravado and therefore they reject the vistas opened up by cloning.

Cloning symbolizes our fear in the face of technological possibilities. By itself it may not be any more frightening than many other technological ventures and yet the symbolism surrounding it places it in a category of its own. While this is cause to take note, it should not constitute the end of the story, since there may also be a positive side to some forms of cloning. This is not assured, but the possibility exists. Understanding is called for.

Control is central to technology

No technological procedure is of interest if it fails to increase human control over human and environmental processes. Such control is the nub of all applied science. But control can be wielded for good or ill, and it is here that cloning comes into the picture. It is the control that is central to human reproductive cloning that is proving so troublesome. The picture so regularly presented is that of making people 'to order', pointing to controlled propagation of human beings. In reality, this is where human reproductive cloning falls down, since the degree of control is far less than indicated by this picture. Clones will not be identical to their progenitors, partly because of the nature of the procedure itself and partly because clones will be exposed to all the vagaries of their environment and culture. And so, the feature of cloning that is proving so terrifying is also its Achilles heel. If we really want to produce people to exact specifications, cloning per se is not the way to go about it.

To do this, one would have to combine cloning with genetic modification, which could – in theory at least – lead to a degree of precision unknown to cloning by itself. The precision could only be attained by altering individual genes, thereby altering the proteins associated with those genes. When this is possible it will lead to precise manipulation of genetic characteristics, and therefore to a previously undreamt of level of control. Would that be something to be deplored? Is control by itself bad? Is it something to be objected to and fought against?

In theory, control could be good, since it could lead to the removal or elimination of serious debilitating diseases. That, surely, would be something to be welcomed. Of course, life may not turn out to be that simple, but it is a possibility that should not be rejected without further analysis.

In spite of such possibilities, the cloning of individuals is an extreme technique that should not be undertaken without extremely careful assessment. This degree of control could prove unwelcome. Even here, though, we need to remind ourselves that control should not be equated with conformity. Simply because human clones would be very similar to existing individuals would not mean they would have to conform to the whims or dictates of those individuals. Any such conformity would be imposed behaviourally; it is not implicit in the cloning itself.

Cloning is a biological procedure; nothing more and nothing less. If it is carried out to diminish individuality and freedom, it is to be condemned. That is social control. But this is not inevitable. As we saw in discussing clowns, eccentricity and difference are to be valued, things that need to be taken into account by genetic engineers. By the same token, they also need to be taken into account by social engineers.

What this shows is that the desire to control is a two-edged sword: while some forms of control may be beneficial, others are to be avoided. In general, precision in the technological area is to be welcomed, whereas social control is dangerous. Differences and individual characteristics are to be encouraged in the midst of precise technological control. This is where wisdom is called for.

Grand designs for human beings are to be treated with the utmost caution, because implicit within them is social control. We are to assess our goals and expectations repeatedly, and these are to be benchmarked against fundamental values from non-technological ages. This is where Christian contributions become relevant, as value systems have to be taken account of and incorporated into technological vistas.

It is imperative that we do not make idols of ourselves or our technology, since such an approach in the cloning area may lead to the worst of technological excesses. Cloning, should it ever be implemented, would constitute a single approach among many. It should never be viewed as an isolated procedure, since that would indeed idolize it and those who set out to clone others. It is because of considerations such as these that cloning needs to be approached within a broader context than the one frequently employed. It is not an end in itself, but one facet of modern medicine. This is undoubtedly jumping the gun, since human reproductive cloning is nowhere near being accepted within society. But the breadth of context is relevant for our future discussion.

Questions for group discussion

1. How realistic do you think the 2060 scenario is?
2. Assuming that the scenario is a realistic one, what might be the advantages and disadvantages of living in such a society?
3. Some people refer to the cloning of human individuals as the unforgivable scientific sin. Discuss this in relation to the dangers of other scientific developments.
4. Discuss the likelihood of Christians accepting some forms of cloning in future years.
5. What do you think is the value of bringing clowns into a discussion of clones?
6. Does the possibility of increasing technological control of human beings concern you? If so, why is this?

Two

And Then There Was Dolly

One could be forgiven for thinking that cloning emerged into the limelight for the first time in February 1997 with the birth of Dolly. Nevertheless, dramatic as that occasion was, it was simply yet another headline-grabbing event along the road to increasingly sophisticated cloning. Perhaps it was the biggest to date, and perhaps in scientific terms it was the most spectacular step forward, but we should not start at this point. To do so would rob us of much of the excitement that is cloning, and particularly human cloning.

It is arbitrary how far back we go, since cloning itself should not be viewed in isolation from numerous other developments in artificial reproduction. Surprisingly, one can go back as far as 1799 to encounter the first report of a pregnancy from artificial insemination. Little dramatic happened in this area for a considerable number of years, until 1944 in fact, when IVF burst on to the laboratory scene. This appears to have set in motion a spate of small developments that would result in the first IVF baby, Louise Brown, in 1978. On the way, sperm was frozen in 1949, the first calf was produced from frozen semen in 1952, and the first human in 1953. Live rabbits were first produced using IVF in 1959, with live mice being obtained from frozen embryos in 1972. Following the birth of Louise Brown, it was just another six years before a baby was born by IVF, following freezing of the embryo.

What is cloning?

The word 'cloning' occurs repeatedly in the scientific literature, since it is used in a number of major ways, only some of which make it into the popular literature. The first usage is *molecular cloning*, where scientists make millions of identical copies of genes. This is of interest to those within the genetic community, and is not the subject of general debate. The second category is *cell cloning*, in which cell lines with identical properties are produced for the study of the biology of specific cells. The third area is that of cloning as it is generally known, although even here there are two subsets. *Embryo splitting* (or the separation of blastomeres) is the artificial division of embryonic cells at a very early stage of development, and replicates the natural process that gives rise to identical twins. For some this is not cloning in the true sense, since identical twins have never been regarded as clones (see below). The second subset is *nuclear replacement/ transfer* (DNA/genomic cloning), that is, cloning in the true sense, namely, the production of a cell or organism with the same nuclear genome as another cell or organism. In other words, cloning is the production of one or more carbon copies of any given cell or whole animal, including human cells or a human individual.

It was in fact the successful cloning of a sheep, the now famous Dolly, in 1997 that represented a major breakthrough in the cloning arena. Dolly's special status stems from the fact that she was the first vertebrate animal to be cloned from a cell of an adult animal as opposed to a cell from an embryo. Dolly the sheep was the brainchild of Ian Wilmut and colleagues at the Roslin Institute in Scotland, in a collaborative effort with PPL Therapeutics. The birth of Dolly provided impetus, and since then cattle, mice and pigs have joined the ranks of clonable animals.

Nuclear replacement involves the introduction of genetic material (a nucleus) into the cytoplasm of an unfertilized egg or embryo, whose own genetic material has been removed. Unlike the embryo splitting technique, nuclear replacement has the potential to create a clone of an adult organism, as was the case with Dolly.

Dolly is an example of what we might call 'sheep reproductive cloning', that is, the cloning of an entire sheep. People do not generally talk about sheep reproductive cloning, because they are not particularly interested in sheep or their clones. What they are interested in is human beings, and so the equivalent in humans is human reproductive cloning, the sort of cloning I discussed in the first chapter. However, as we shall see shortly, there is also another category of cloning, *human therapeutic cloning*, where nuclear transplantation is being employed to produce tissues rather than complete individuals. It will also become obvious that I think this latter form of cloning is infinitely more important than the cloning of individuals. This is because the production of tissues and cell lines has far more potential for the treatment of disease, that is, for clinical medicine and for healing people. One problem, though, is that different terms are used for this technique, since it is sometimes called somatic cell nuclear replacement (or transfer; SCNT) rather than human therapeutic cloning.

There are various potential uses of cloning techniques and a discussion of these will help to identify both the scientific and ethical issues involved. From a scientific viewpoint, cloning opens up numerous potential research and therapeutic opportunities. For example, it may increase our understanding of the fundamental processes of cellular differentiation, thereby making possible its reversal, and hence providing a means of controlling pathological and aging processes. Cloning technology also has the potential to improve the efficiency of production of transgenic livestock: which could be used both for the production of organs or tissues for transplantation into humans, and for the production of human proteins in cow's or goat's milk. This, in turn, illustrates the pharmaceutical possibilities opened up by some uses of cloning technologies.

But we are jumping well ahead of ourselves. This is the future, and before we tackle the future we should look closely at how we have arrived at the gates to the future. Where has cloning come from? What has led up to where we are today?

Frustrated attempts at cloning

Embryologists (or as some people tend to call them today, developmental biologists) are interested in the very earliest stages of an animal's development. Once fertilization has taken place, what are the processes involved in converting a fertilized egg into a fully formed animal? Complex as this is, it is possible to map out the various processes involved, a task that has proved both frustrating and demanding, and that is still far from complete. Although the issues here are far wider than those involved in cloning, cloning does, as we shall see, take us right into the middle of some very crucial debates about development.

As the nineteenth century turned into the twentieth, a number of embryologists were intensely interested in cell division and in the way in which cells undergo differentiation to become specialized cells and tissues. One of these, Hans Driesch, working with sea-urchin embryos, found that he could shake apart the cells of, first, two-cell embryos, and then four-cell embryos. These then produced two and four embryos respectively. Looking back, one can say that this was probably the first successful example of cloning in the laboratory, and yet Driesch was not concerned about cloning. His interest was in the nature of cell differentiation, as he sought to discover whether totipotency (the ability of a cell to form a whole embryo) is lost as cleavage proceeds.

This was taken further by another German biologist, Hans Spemann, in the early part of the twentieth century, when he separated the two blastomeres of salamander embryos, and noted that each developed into a whole embryo. This demonstrated that the blastomeres of two-cell amphibian embryos do indeed retain totipotency.

Around the same time, the German-American, Jacques Loeb, induced sea-urchin eggs to develop parthenogenetically, that is, without fertilization. He managed to simulate fertilization by altering the chemical composition of the sea water in which the eggs were kept, which proved sufficiently disruptive to imitate penetration of the egg by a sperm. The unfertilized egg cell began to divide to produce embryos that sometimes developed well.

Among other things, he demonstrated that embryonic cells retain totipotency even after they have undergone several divisions.

Spemann, working again with salamanders, succeeded with a form of nuclear transfer by forcing nuclei from relatively mature cytoplasm into cytoplasm retaining the properties of the original egg. Following this, in 1938, he proposed an experiment that he considered 'fantastical', to take the nucleus from a differentiated cell and place it in the cytoplasm of an egg whose own nucleus had been removed (an enucleated egg). This experiment was never undertaken by him, and yet with hindsight it is precisely what SCNT is all about.

Later, in the 1950s, Robert Briggs in Philadelphia set out to determine whether as differentiation proceeds genes are shut down rather than lost altogether. Working with frogs, he and Thomas J. King succeeded in bringing about nuclear transfer, and showed that the cell nuclei of blastulae (young embryos) well past the two- or four-cell stage retained totipotency. They had managed to initiate the cloning process in frogs, although, as with all others working in this field, their interest was in cell differentiation and not in cloning per se. A little later, John Gurdon in Oxford was able to demonstrate that some of the nuclei from tadpole intestinal cells could produce whole embryos when transferred into enucleated *Xenopus* egg cytoplasm. Some of these embryos became tadpoles and some even turned into fertile frogs. Quite clearly, he had shown that some specialized cells retain totipotency, although he concluded that the more specialized transferred cells are, the less likely they are to support frog development beyond the early stages. This idea from the 1960s remained one of the central tenets of cloning biology until the mid-1990s.

In other words, it has long been known that nuclei from very early embryonic frog tadpoles can be transplanted into eggs to produce viable adults. On the other hand, nuclei from mature tadpoles or adult frogs were less successful, since the cloned animals developed only as far as the tadpole stage before dying. Not only this, frogs and salamanders are not mammals, and if people want to translate science into serious technology, and apply what is known to agriculture and human medicine (as Ian Wilmut and colleagues did), then it is imperative to work with mammals. The cloning of amphibians is only a step on the way to something far more dramatic – and ultimately far more useful.

Cloning in mammals is far more difficult for a host of reasons, including the very small size of their eggs, and the fact that all aspects of reproduction take place inside the body. What this demanded scientifically was the elaboration of a whole new range of techniques.

In 1981 it seemed as if this had been achieved with a paper in the journal *Cell*, when Karl Illmensee and Peter Hoppe at the University of Geneva announced the birth of three mice cloned by nuclear transfer. The donor nuclei had been taken from relatively advanced embryos and had been introduced into enucleated eggs using microsurgery. It appeared to be a brilliant breakthrough. Unfortunately, other scientists were unable to repeat this work using exactly the same methods, despite repeated and very careful attempts. There were two consequences: the study of Illmensee and Hoppe was discredited, and the scientists who had tried so hard to replicate their work uttered a resounding statement: 'the cloning of mammals, by simple nuclear transfer, is biologically impossible'.[1] In other words, cloning as we normally use the term today is impossible. This 1984 statement probably hindered research in this sector of developmental biology, marginalizing cloning as a serious scientific area to study. Grants became extremely difficult to obtain, and it gradually faded from the scene in the high-profile world of molecular biology. But it also proved an assertion that others set out to disprove, even if this was in the neglected world of animal science. It was in these laboratories, where scientists were motivated by commercially useful agricultural and pharmaceutical projects rather than by laboratory animals mimicking human

---

[1] J. McGrath and D. Stolter, 'Inability of Mouse Blastomere Nuclei Transferred to Enucleated Zygotes to Support Development *In Vitro*', 1317–18.

diseases, that the road towards cloning was laid. Their interest in sheep, pigs and cattle represented a completely different world from that of the biologists interested in mice.

Advances between the mid-1980s and 1990s involved some very erudite work on phenomena such as genome activation, genomic imprinting, and the cell cycle. The details of these are well beyond our interests in this book, and yet they should impress upon us the seriousness of the science and the brilliance of the intellectual breakthroughs, both of which were vital before cloning could be accomplished in mammals. What we have here is not an example of spurious bravado or humanistic hubris, but scientific advances of quite a profound character. One example will suffice: the time when genes are switched on in the young embryo is crucial, and it emerged that in cattle and humans this is at the eight-cell stage.

In 1985 Steen Willadsen became the first biologist to clone sheep. While his techniques were to be improved upon a few years later, he had succeeded, whereas attempts to clone mice had failed. His cloning started with cells from embryos, and his paper in *Nature* concluded with these words: 'It seems reasonable to suggest that a firm basis has been established for further experiments involving nuclear transplantation in large domestic species.'[2] A little after this, cattle were cloned from eight- and sixteen-cell embryos in the United States, but despite considerable successes there were practical problems that prevented the cattle-cloning program from establishing itself as a viable technology.

This brings us virtually up to date with the cloning program that was to result in Dolly, but I want to digress a little before returning to it.

---

[2] S.M. Willadsen, 'Nuclear Transfer in Sheep Embryos', 63–5.

Cloning in the public eye

Initial ethical debate

The recent history of cloning in the public arena has been a murky one, the fear and fascination of this procedure leading to some bizarre events. Perhaps I can begin in 1963 when J.B.S. Haldane, doyen of British biologists, speculated on the cloning experiments then going on in frogs. In a talk with the provocative title 'Biological possibilities for the human species over the next ten thousand years' he foresaw that cloning would be a boon, enabling humans to control their own evolution. By cloning the brightest people, we would increase the number of great thinkers, artists, athletes and beauties in the population. In this way, Haldane speculated, we would dramatically increase human achievement. For Haldane the clones of geniuses would lead us into a better world.

These rampant speculations were followed in 1966 by a better-informed vision, when the well-known geneticist and commentator on human evolution, Joshua Lederberg, wrote an article in *The American Naturalist* entitled 'Experimental genetics and human evolution'. Among the topics covered in that perceptive article on the genetic basis of many facets of modern society, he discussed nuclear transplantation, calling it 'clonal reproduction'. The context within which he was working was quite different from ours, since he was interested in efficient ways of controlling human nature. He wanted to influence social policy through the application of genetics. At one point Lederberg wrote, 'If a superior individual is identified, why not copy it directly, rather than suffer all the risks of recombinational disruption, including those of sex'[3]. He showed considerable foresight in recognizing the advantages of cloning for overcoming rejection problems in organ transplantation. On the other hand, he also foresaw clones being able to communicate more easily with one another; a far more dubious prediction. More ominously, when contemplating

---

[3] J. Lederberg, 'Experimental Genetics and Human Evolution', 527.

broader social objectives, Lederberg slid into the realm of somewhat bizarre science fiction, seriously proposing the possible production of subhuman hybrids. His approach was that of the social engineer attempting to influence cultural evolution, rather than of the health professional attempting to improve the lot of ordinary individuals. In this regard, his article has a distant feel to it, reminding us that even ideas on cloning have undergone substantial changes over the past thirty years or so. We should bear this in mind when studying the responses to cloning over recent years.

In 1972 Willard Gaylin, one of the founders of the Hastings Center in New York, the pivotal bioethics establishment, wrote an article on cloning to garner attention to the issues arising out of modern biology. With the chilling title 'The Frankenstein myth becomes a reality – We have the awful knowledge to make exact copies of human beings', he called the readers of *The New York Times Magazine* to treat the possibility of cloning seriously. He challenged people to think seriously about so-called value-free science, and about the need to take ethics seriously. On the other hand, he was well aware that clones might not be like their original, and he was sufficiently perceptive to comment that a genetic Saint Francis clone could evolve into a tyrant, and a Hitler clone could have the potential for sainthood.

About a decade later, in 1981, the Roman Catholic theologian Richard McCormick viewed cloning entirely in eugenic terms. His discussion was in the context of a procedure that would have as its goal the removal of deleterious genetic material from the gene pool, and programming of the genotype in such a way as to maximize certain desirable traits, notably: intelligence, creativity, and artistic ability. He was not alone in this – and he is not to be criticized for these emphases – but it is instructive since this was the context within which the whole debate was being carried out at that time. Unfortunately, very strong remnants of this debate have carried over into far more recent debate, even though the science of cloning is of a different ilk.

One of the reasons why Lederberg's 1966 article proved important was because it elicited responses from two well-known theologians of the time, Paul Ramsey and Joseph

Fletcher. Their debate revolved around human freedom, embodiment, our relationship with nature, and the meaning of parenthood. Historic as this particular debate is, it illustrates very clearly two different approaches to biomedical technology. As one traces one's steps through the debate, one encounters surprisingly modern issues. This is undoubtedly because Fletcher's humanistic idealism gave the impression that science could achieve almost everything, and that what mattered above all else was quality control. Like Lederberg, he lacked the far more cautious aspects of today's scientific debate. For Fletcher there is no ethical objection to cloning when it is used morally, the criteria for what is moral being determined subjectively.

In contrast to Fletcher's emphasis on mastery over nature, Ramsey was far more aware that technology can mean power for some people over others, and possibly not for their good. What would clones think if they had been produced for some socially dangerous task? Fletcher seemed to care little as long as the task could be justified as being in society's interests; not so Ramsey. Ramsey rejected any technology that exploited a dualism in our relationship between ourselves and our bodies; for him the person is an embodied soul or an ensouled body. Any technology that separates what we are as people from what we are as bodies should be rejected. Therefore, any form of reproductive technology involving the manipulation of embryos should be rejected. For Ramsey a child is neither a human achievement nor a product, but a gift of God. His apprehension about the intrusion of technology into the act of procreation carried over into cloning, and placed him implacably against such ventures – even though they lay in the future at the time he was writing in the 1960s and 1970s.

While Fletcher appeared to have little interest in the voices of the cloned, Ramsey was deeply concerned with the voiceless in any human experimentation. Perhaps the contrast between the two is too great, in that both represented extreme positions difficult to incorporate into contemporary debate. Nevertheless, they point to important trends for us today. Fletcher reminds us that we cannot escape the tension between chance and control, whereas Ramsey points out the importance of caution and humility in the face of what may appear to be overwhelming scientific enthusiasm and brashness. Unfortunately, the next chapter in the cloning debate was far less helpful.

This was the well-known episode in 1978 when David Rorvik, a science journalist, wrote a book, *In His Image,* claiming to be an account of the events leading up to the first birth by cloning of a human being. According to this account, an American millionaire in his sixties wanted to leave to posterity a clone of himself. In order to do this he enlisted David Rorvik to find a biologist willing to work on the project in complete secrecy and with unlimited finances. Despite a chasm of unknowns, the work from the start utilized humans. Conveniently, the laboratory was situated in some undisclosed, idyllic-sounding paradise where there was little difficulty in obtaining women 'volunteers'. Conveniently, these 'volunteers' were not informed of the nature of the experiments and, during their dubious hospital stay, eggs were obtained from them. A few of the women acted as surrogate mothers to carry eggs cloned with cells from the donor millionaire. Eventually, one of them carried a clone to term, and was apparently living with the millionaire and his one-year-old clone son towards the end of 1977.

This book was denounced as a fraud, and in 1982 one of the scientists mentioned in it won a legal suit against Rorvik and the publishers on the grounds that he had never engaged in, or advocated, the cloning of a human being. Finally, the publishers conceded that they believed the story to be untrue. This blurring of fact and fiction highlights the shadowy world long associated with cloning.

Looking back to the early 1980s it is significant that discussion of the ethical issues raised by cloning was largely dismissed because cloning was regarded as scientifically unrealistic. In other words, it was not considered worth debating. As a result, far less attention was given to the arguments surrounding cloning than might have been expected. Even the President's Commission for the Study of Ethical Problems in Medicine and Biomedical and Behavioral Research, in the United States in

1982, fell into this trap. This is the reason why a report in that year, *Splicing Life: The Social and Ethical Issues of Genetic Engineering with Human Beings,* dismissed it.

In spite of this, some important articles appeared in the ethics literature in the mid-1980s. For instance, Martin LaBar, writing in 1984, provided cogent reasons why cloning would not lessen the worth of genetically identical individuals. He realized even then that clones would not resemble each other as much as identical twins do, because the cytoplasm of eggs affects development. He also noted that identical twins have distinctively different personalities. Another writer came to the same conclusion on the ground that human beings differ from one another because of their unique pattern of roles and relationships. However, the paucity of useful results in numerous cloning endeavours in the prestigious world of reproductive biology meant that little scientific attention was paid to cloning as a serious possibility in mammals until the early 1990s.

Ethical debate in the early 1990s

It was at this time that cloning again hit the headlines. In November 1993, *Time* magazine wrote at length about the duplication of human embryos. What was dubbed a landmark experiment consisted of duplicating abnormal human embryos by separating the constituent cells at the two-cell stage and enabling these two resulting cells (blastomeres) to develop into embryos. This is what I referred to earlier as embryo splitting (or the separation of blastomeres). The work was carried out by Jerry Hall and colleagues at George Washington University and was presented at a meeting of the American Fertility Society. This is what happens when identical twins are created naturally, and is not accepted as true cloning by some authorities. None of the 'clones' grew for more than six days in the laboratory since they were abnormal. The scientific community placed little stress on this work but for a short period the media placed great store by it.

A *Time*/CNN poll at the time suggested that 75 per cent of Americans found the idea of human cloning troubling, 40 per cent would have put a temporary halt on this research, and 46 per cent favoured a law making it a crime to clone a human being. Various dignitaries reacted with horror, and considered the experiment unthinkable. *Time* itself referred to the crossing of a line, the breaking of a taboo, while in even more picturesque language reference was made to cookie-cutter humans, baked and bred to order; baby farming was on the horizon, and clones cannibalized for spare parts were envisaged. For some it was regarded as the dawn of the eugenics era, and yet others warned that scientific misunderstanding can generate unwarranted fears and spontaneous overreactions. Their concern was that if we focus attention on wild and improbable scenarios, we will precipitate mindless debate. The public reaction to a relatively unexceptional scientific experiment was a harbinger of what was to come a few years later.

However, it was not only the popular media that gave considerable attention to this experiment. In 1994 serious bioethics journals, such as the *Kennedy Institute of Ethics Journal* and the *Hastings Center Report*, devoted many pages to this form of cloning, that is, the separation of blastomeres. This is not cloning in any revolutionary form, and looking back on it nearly ten years later one wonders what all the fuss was about.

It may have been unfortunate that the word 'cloning' was used in the title of the talk and abstract, since it appears to have been this that elicited so much interest and overreaction. Nevertheless, the separation of blastomeres can be accommodated under the umbrella of cloning, albeit in a broad sense, since if cloning covers identical replication and the production of a duplicate copy, this is cloning. However, it is not cloning in the most interesting sense of taking the nucleus of a body cell and transferring it to an unfertilized egg.

With hindsight it is fascinating to reflect that the reasons given in favour of embryo splitting were to enhance the chances of pregnancy, within the context of IVF procedures. Justification for this procedure was that it was not cloning of the nuclear transplantation variety. One wonders whether this was merely a smokescreen, although some commentators doubted if such procedures could be confined to embryo splitting. Amazingly though, others used this very limited technique to envision armies of identical individuals being produced for all sorts of mundane tasks. All one can say is that embryo splitting would be an exceedingly inefficient way of achieving this grand design. Fortunately, this was recognized at the time by a number of writers.

Modest as this experiment was, some of the ethical issues that would surface a few years later were being rehearsed at this time. These revolved around the presumed loss of individual uniqueness, the possibility of causing harm to the interests of the child, the creation of embryos for the purpose of genetic diagnosis, and public policy issues. What is interesting is the usefulness of some of this debate, especially in the hands of those who seriously questioned the basis of these objections. While these issues do not concern us here, it is instructive to listen to those who asked for clear thinking. For instance, it is insufficient to claim that making copies of individuals lessens their worth, or to state that we have a right to our own individual genetic identity. Worthy as such claims may sound, we have to ask whether they can be supported by convincing arguments. Why should two copies of someone lessen their worth? Does this apply to identical twins? From where does the 'right' to genetic uniqueness arise? If there is such a right, against whom are identical twins to complain that their right has been removed from them? One also has to ask how the interests of the child are harmed by splitting blastomeres. It is true that harms may be caused by expecting the child to live up to clearly defined expectations as seen in an already existing clone born a number of years previously (an identical 'twin' in a different generation). But this is nothing more than an extreme instance of what may happen under any situation where a naturally conceived child is expected to live up to parental expectations.

In the United States the National Advisory Board on Ethics in Reproduction (NABER) held a workshop on cloning. Their main concerns were with the following questions: Why would anyone want to clone humans? Will cloning fundamentally injure our conception of what it means to be human? Will cloning negatively affect individual identity and uniqueness? Will the anticipated biological and social effects of cloning have a beneficial or detrimental effect on our underlying ethical framework and social fabric? I shall not follow these arguments here since they will come up in the next chapter and they deal with true cloning and not simply with blastomere separation. What stands out is that the arguments have remained constant over the years.

One helpful debate took place between John A. Robertson and Richard McCormick in the pages of the *Hastings Center Report* in 1994. Both took embryo splitting seriously. Robertson's approach was governed by the prospects of assisting infertile couples, while McCormick's concentrated far more on the potential of the early embryo for personhood. For McCormick, embryo manipulation held the prospect of affecting personal and social attitudes towards human life. For him, embryo splitting would lead to a further erosion of respect, since it was a form of preferential breeding. This would lead us to value people by the traits they exhibit, and not by what they are as people in their wholeness. Once we do this, we open the way, he thought, to doing unacceptable things to the debilitated, retarded, elderly and marginalized. We will make parental acceptance conditional on the quality and acceptability of the child in biological terms, an attitude that is the antithesis of unconditional love.

McCormick's concerns extended way beyond blastomere splitting. As he looked ahead, he saw even this technique as harming all of us – and not just cloned individuals – because our wonder at human diversity and individuality will be shattered. He viewed with fear the temptation to collapse the human person into genetic data, while the mere possibility of human cloning would, he thought, change both us and our sense of the sanctity, wholeness and individuality of human life. The consequences of such temerarious temptations were not worked out by McCormick, and I shall return to them in the next chapter.

On the road to Dolly

This digression must seem a long way from the scientific work I was describing previously, and in effect the two are far removed from each other. This is very important for us to remember. It is all too easy to skip the serious science and jump immediately to the science fiction, to evade the quiet revolution taking place in the laboratory for the excitement of the horror stories and the grand plans of illusory mad pseudo-scientists. The transition from science to philosophy or theology is generally made far too quickly, thereby overlooking the reasons why this type of work is being conducted and ignoring the nature of the goals in view. This may sometimes be an unfortunate oversight, but on other occasions I get the feeling that it is at best slipshod reasoning and at worst a dishonest manipulation of the scientific enterprise.

It should have become evident by now that a quiet revolution was taking place in a few agricultural research laboratories, far away from the limelight of the intensely competitive university research laboratories using routine laboratory animals. It was in the agricultural laboratories that the progress was being made, spurred on by the technological prospects held out within the agricultural domain. As an understanding of fundamental cellular processes increased step by step in the Roslin laboratories outside Edinburgh, so a succession of cloned sheep came on the scene. Each group represented a step forward from the last.

The first group appeared in 1989, and while the science had much in common with what had gone before, it established the Roslin Institute as a serious centre of cloning. It also showed that nuclear transfer is successful not just from eight- or sixteen-cell embryos, but also from a later stage: from the blastocyst and from cells of its inner cell mass, at which time the genome has been activated. Even more significantly, Ian Wilmut and co-workers realized that what is of critical importance for cloning is the cell cycle – particularly that of the donor cell. This was *the* major breakthrough that was required, and once that had been made much else fell into place.

It was developments along these lines that resulted in a pivotal paper in *Nature* in March 1996, 'Sheep cloned by nuclear transfer from a cultured cell line'. This reported the birth of two sheep known affectionately in the Roslin laboratory as Megan and Morag. It is interesting that Ian Wilmut regards these sheep, born in August 1995, as the true pioneers since with their birth the new age of biotechnology commenced. This is because the techniques used in their case were the ones that would usher in the new age of cloning. Megan and Morag had been produced from embryos, rather than from adult cells, and so another major step was still awaited. And yet what they signified was that differentiated mammalian cells can be reprogrammed; simple as this sounds it marks the overturning of a deeply entrenched dogma in developmental biology. This was a breakthrough of quite immense proportions, so immense that it is difficult to stress the point too strongly.

Up to that point scientists had been aware of the significance of the degree of differentiation of the donor cells, the nature of the cells, and how many times the cells had divided in culture. What people like Ian Wilmut, Keith Campbell and others came to realize was that the success or failure of cloning is determined mainly by the stage of the donor cell cycle. The cycle has to be in the Go, the quiescent stage, since this is the stage when the genome can be reprogrammed. In addition, the state of the recipient egg is also of importance. It was this shift in emphasis from the degree of differentiation to the cell cycle that made mammalian cloning feasible. Regardless of any ethical issues with cloning, one should acknowledge the remarkable insights that, over a period of a few years, made this step possible.

Looking back on the magnitude of this scientific achievement, one might have expected an enormous amount of media interest in the publication of the 1996 paper. While there was some, after an initial flurry of interest, the paper elicited little debate in the public arena. Perhaps it was overshadowed by the tragic events in Dunblane with the shooting of school children, or perhaps the startling scientific significance was missed. Either way, it was studiously ignored by everyone other than a small number of aficionados.

Consequently, the world was taken by surprise when in February 1997 the article 'Viable offspring derived from fetal and adult mammalian cells', by the same research group, appeared in *Nature*. Strictly speaking, the epochal event happened three days earlier, when the findings were prematurely disclosed by a British newspaper, and Dolly (the cloned lamb) was presented to the public. Although Ian Wilmut does not consider Dolly as interesting scientifically as Megan or Morag, nor some other sheep that followed, she was the first animal to be created from cultured, differentiated cells taken from an adult. She convincingly demonstrated that cells committed to the tasks of adulthood can be reprogrammed to become totipotent again; they can give rise to other cell types and in a sense start life all over again.

The events surrounding Dolly's conception are well known, one might even say legendary. What Wilmut and co-workers did was to transplant the nucleus from an adult body cell (from the udder) of an adult sheep into an enucleated egg of another sheep. The new egg with its donor nucleus was stimulated and responded just as if it had been fertilized: the resulting lamb was genetically identical to the adult sheep from which the nucleus had come. In spite of uncertainties at the time (it took 277 attempts to produce Dolly; it was doubted how long Dolly would survive, and whether she would age prematurely) what was far more significant was that a mature mammalian cell has the capacity to differentiate. For all intents and purposes this cell should have remained a sheep's udder cell. However, by appropriate manipulation, the nuclear material reprogrammed itself so that it could again differentiate.

Dolly is what is sometimes referred to as a genomic clone or a DNA clone. This means that she is not identical to the ewe from which the nucleus came. The cytoplasm from which she developed is that of the host egg. Unfortunately, many cloning commentators have missed this point, but it is a highly significant one. For example, the mitochondria in the cytoplasm cannot be overlooked, and they may be of considerable consequence for the resulting animal; the details have to be worked out now that cloned animals are in existence.

Dolly was quickly followed by other cloned sheep, since various series of experiments were being conducted at Roslin at the same time. All those early sheep had delightful names. The next to mention are Cedric, Cecil, Cyril and Tuppence, cloned from cultured embryo cells. Then there were Taffy and Tweed from cultured fetal fibroblasts, showing that these very general cells may prove a convenient way of cloning – with enormous implications for the production of cloned animals for agricultural purposes.

Later came Polly, probably the most exciting sheep of all from this era at Roslin. Polly had been cloned from fetal fibroblasts, but had also been genetically transformed – being fitted with a gene for human factor IX. With this birth, pharming came of age. Pharming is the name given to the process by which therapeutically valuable materials such as proteins can be produced within genetically modified livestock. In the case of Polly it was factor IX, a protein that contributes to blood clotting. The gene for this factor was added to the early embryo, so that when Polly grew up, the gene product (factor IX) was present in Polly's milk from which it can subsequently be extracted. Tracy, yet another sheep, but not cloned on this occasion, had been genetically modified to produce alpha-1-antitrypsin (AAT; an enzyme which maintains the correct elasticity of the lungs and is deficient in those with cystic fibrosis) in her milk.

At the time of the publication of news of Dolly's birth, there was scepticism in some quarters that Dolly had actually come from an adult cell. The evidence produced at the time supported Wilmut, and yet a doubt remained in the minds of some. This was dispelled completely in mid-1998 when fifty cloned mice were produced from adult cells. With these births and the imminent arrival of cloned calves and pigs, cloning was indeed a real phenomenon. Not only this, DNA analyses proved that Dolly and the ewe she was cloned from are genetically identical, as would be expected of clones.

At this point it is pertinent to ask a question: Should any of this cloning work have been stopped for ethical reasons? The degree of alarm expressed since the birth of Dolly forces us to ask this question. If cloning is as bad as many claim it to be, why was there not considerable clamour at some step along the road to Dolly? After all, none of the work had been carried out in secret. It had all been published openly in respected international journals. Even the highly significant paper announcing the birth of Megan and Morag had elicited hardly a stir – certainly the ethicists remained largely silent. As we have already seen, cloning had been debated on and off for many years, and while there had been serious ethical debate at times, in the latter years the silence had been almost palpable. Even now most attention is focused on cloning itself, rather than on genetic modification which is perhaps a far more powerful technique. But this is to jump the gun.

Nevertheless, the questions I have posed here point to an unpalatable fact: namely, that many commentators fail to understand how science or scientists work. The intense drive to understand natural processes, and the parallel desire to control these processes, are fundamental to science. Generally, they are not headline-grabbing ones: those are what politicians, the media, and social planners think about. The goals of scientists are to find out more about growth factors, enzymes and exocytosis – not the stuff of four-centimetre-high front-page titles. But such esoteric interests fuel the huge advances in medicine and biotechnology, and occasionally give rise to phenomena like cloning.

The biotechnology revolution

From a scientific viewpoint, the cloning of *animals* opens up numerous potential research and therapeutic opportunities. For example, using cloned experimental animals may well increase our understanding of the fundamental processes of cellular differentiation, thereby making possible its reversal, and hence providing a means of controlling pathological and aging processes. Cloning technology also has the potential to improve the efficiency of the production of transgenic livestock, which could be used both for the production of tissues or organs for transplantation into humans, as well as the production of human proteins in cow's or goat's milk. As we have just seen, Polly – the transgenic sheep – ushered in the new era, however tentative it may be at this early stage. What it does tell us, though, is that the pharmaceutical possibilities of developments such as this are enticing and far reaching, utilizing as they do cloning allied with genetic modification. It is this combination that provides the real powerhouse of cloning.

The work of people like Ian Wilmut, Keith Campbell and others is, in my view, intensely serious and responsible work. It is an illustration of science at its best, with an ardent desire to understand better fundamental developmental processes; it also illustrates technology at its best: how agricultural and pharmaceutical processes can be improved. This work and that of many forerunners is far removed from the scaremongering of some policymakers and even academics. Wilmut and colleagues had no interest in cloning as a procedure in its own right; they were not aiming to be the first to clone a mammal for the mere sake of the kudos this would bring. They carried out cloning for a far more mundane reason – as a means by which to study differentiation in early development.

What is fascinating is that this work by itself would elicit little, if any, interest outside the scientific community. It is difficult to imagine ethicists, policymakers, theologians or any of the other host of professionals who write about cloning, having the slightest concern about the differentiation of cells. The spectre of cloning, though, transforms the science and technology of research laboratories and pharmaceutical companies into headline news of forbidding dimensions. They cannot be blamed entirely for this, but it should serve as an amber light, making us at least stop and ask whether our interpretation of the science is as accurate as we have assumed.

The science I have been describing has nothing to do with the cloning of humans. Indeed, Ian Wilmut has repeatedly expressed his own opposition to human reproductive cloning. While he may or may not be representative of developmental biologists as a group, the thrust and drive behind cloning techniques stem from their intrinsic scientific interest and from their technological implications for agriculture. While these have to be assessed on their own terms, they should impress upon us that the dimensions of the debate have nothing inherently to do with the cloning of human individuals. Any social or theological implications of cloning procedures should also take these dimensions into account.

This, then, is an exceedingly important context for the debate, all too often overlooked especially by social and ethical commentators. But it does not mean we are let off the hook, nor that cloning does not have any serious implications. It does. As Wilmut and Campbell say, 'It is as if the science and techniques of biology have been liberated from constraints that once seemed inviolable. We and our descendants must wait and see what the world makes of this liberation – or rather, must try to see that the new power is put only to good and proper use.' And again: 'It would be dangerous ever to suppose that we can understand all of life's processes exhaustively: this would lead us into the Greek sin of hubris, with all the penalties that follow. Yet our descendants will find themselves with power that seems limited only by their imagination.'[4]

For some, these will seem frightening prospects, and yet they were not written with that intention. They are straightforward extrapolations from the science that is currently taking place. They are not suggesting that certain paths must be taken, but simply that certain directions are now open to us, directions that remind us of the power shortly to be placed in the hands of humans. Remember, the power which these scientists are speaking about is not the power to create armies of human slaves (which would be as unrealistic as it would be barbaric), but the power to provide precise control over the development of farm animals. The detailed reasons for doing this are beyond the scope of this book, but they revolve around the following:

- laboratory research: producing genetically identical animal strains without inbreeding

---

[4] I. Wilmut, et al., *The Second Creation*, 267.

- replicating elite farm livestock
- animal conservation
- cloning with genetic transformation: pharming (as in the case of Polly)
- cloning tissues (see Chapter 4)
- xenotransplantation: using organs from other species (e.g. pigs) for transplantation into humans, and producing transgenic animals containing appropriate human genes to minimize organ rejection
- production of disease-resistant livestock
- combining cloning with genomics and gene targeting, which will only emerge when all the genes of a species have been mapped and their functions known

Listing possibilities like this will cause some people to become even more worried about cloning and its implications. What we do have here is some idea of the likely and exceedingly useful (the first four), those that may directly involve humans (the next two), and those currently in the realms of science fiction (the last two). On the other hand, a list of this ilk does not justify any of the possibilities.

Besides these, there are numerous questions for the scientific community of the future, including: How are the various bits of DNA turned on and off in each cell type as the organism unfolds? What tells the genes to switch on in the developing embryo? How is it possible to reprogram a genome and are there limits to reprogramming? What is the action of any particular gene, and to what extent is that action influenced by other genes, and by the cellular environment? These are profound questions, and answers will probably not be forthcoming rapidly or easily, but at least they can be asked seriously.

But why should we be interested in these questions? Most of us will never be in a position to contribute to answers, and we may not be the slightest bit interested in that anyway. The reason is that as our understanding along these lines increases, it leads to increasing control over fundamental biological processes, regardless of what animals these are in. Control in these instances may be exercised by permanently altering the genes that underpin various developmental processes, or the development of drugs specifically designed to influence particular genes. In these ways, it may prove possible to come up with drugs to help fetuses develop in a healthy fashion. When things go wrong, it may prove possible to direct cells to produce the tissues required to aid healing. The revolution currently under way is hard to overemphasize, since cloning has already shown that genes that have been shut down can be switched on again. The early developmental processes appear to be far more pliable than conventionally thought. To quote Wilmut and Campbell again, 'There will always be deficiencies and inconsistencies. Biology will never come to an end. But for practical purposes we might as well assume that absolute control will be possible ... We are entering the age of biological control, and we should gird our moral and political loins accordingly.'[5]

This could be construed as being sensationalist. But is it? Another way of expressing much the same is to suggest that cloning applied to human beings (not necessarily human reproductive cloning) could be achieved by 2014. Wilmut has suggested this, not because he agrees with it – he does not – but to demonstrate what he regards as the speed with which science and scientific ideas are moving.

The explosion that was Dolly

The birth of Dolly was seen by many as shocking. So shocking, in fact, that *Nature*, the journal that published the epochal paper, received an email prior to publication urging it to withdraw publication for fear that the technique would be abused.

As so often happens, *Time* magazine encapsulated much of the feeling with the headline introductory sentence to its special report on cloning in its 10 March 1997 issue: 'One doesn't expect Dr Frankenstein to show up in wool sweater, baggy

---

[5] Ibid., 288.

parker, soft British accent and the face of a bank clerk.' Ian Wilmut was the man, the deceptively ordinary man – not the forbidding white-coated scientist, but Dr Frankenstein nevertheless. To quote *Time* again, he was 'the first man to create fully formed life from adult body parts since Mary Shelley's mad scientist'. In picturesque language, *Time* continued, 'And what hath Wilmut wrought? A fully formed, perfectly healthy mammal ... born from a single cell. Not since God took Adam's rib and fashioned a helpmate for him has anything so fantastic occurred'.

The biblical proportions of the event shine eloquently through. Even the language has to be that of the King James Version. The journalistic hyperbole directs our attention to the apparent theological overtones of what had taken place. 'Man' had grown; 'he' had become a creator, rivalling only God. The lines of battle had been drawn; the conflict between science and faith was staring us in the face. None of this may be true, but the pictorial language and imagery prove just as forbidding as the term 'cloning' itself.

Gina Kolata also grasped for theological language when confronted by cloning. She wrote

> We live in a time when sin is becoming one of those quaint words that we might hear in church but that has little to do with our daily world. Cloning, however, with its possibilities for creating our own identical twins, brings us back to the ancient sins of vanity and pride.

Is there a hidden fear that we would be forcing God to give us another soul, thereby bending God to our will, or, worse yet, that we would be creating soulless beings that were merely genetic shells of humans?[6]

One could describe in almost endless detail the metaphors used and the hype purveyed by headline after headline: 'Well, Hello Dolly', 'Dolly is just cloning around', 'Double trouble', 'Clone the clowns', 'An udder way of making lambs', and so on. Public figures were quick to denounce cloning people as

---

[6]   G. Kolata, *Clone: The Road to Dolly, and the Path Ahead*, 5–6.

repugnant, unacceptable, a horrendous crime, a xeroxing of souls. In the United States 74 per cent in one public opinion poll answered that it is against God's will to clone human beings; in another, 87 per cent said that human cloning should not be allowed. In a number of countries various penalties were suggested for anyone attempting to clone a human. However, as the debate progressed it became increasingly clear that a distinction had to be made between cellular-level cloning for research purposes, and cloning with the aim of producing a human individual.

Perhaps the most forthright declaration came from the European Parliament, with its 12 March 1997 resolution calling for a ban on human cloning. This was based on its view that human cloning 'is a serious violation of fundamental human rights and is contrary to the principle of equality of human beings as it permits a eugenic and racist selection of the human race, it offends against human dignity and it requires experimentation on human beings'. It also stressed that each individual has a right to his or her own genetic identity. The General Assembly of the World Health Organization (WHO) adopted a resolution affirming that human cloning is contrary to human integrity and morality. The 186 member states of the United Nations Educational, Scientific and Cultural Organization (UNESCO) unanimously passed a declaration towards the end of 1997 calling for a cloning ban.

A protocol to the Council of Europe's Bioethics Convention was signed by seventeen countries in early 1998 prohibiting any attempt to create a human being genetically identical to another human being, whether living or dead. Their reasoning was as follows:

Deliberately cloning humans is a threat to human identity, as it would give up the indispensable protection against the predetermination of the human genetic constitution by a third party ... human dignity ... is endangered by instrumentalization through artificial human cloning ... As naturally occurring genetic recombination is likely to create more freedom for the human being than a predetermined genetic make-up, it is in the interest of all persons to keep the essentially random nature of the composition of their genes.

The National Bioethics Advisory Commission (NBAC) in the United States produced a report in June 1997, in response to a request from the President. It recommended that in the short term there should be a continuation of the moratorium on the use of federal funding in support of any attempt to create a child by SCNT (human reproductive cloning) and an immediate request to the private sector to comply voluntarily with the intent of the federal moratorium. The reasons given concerned, firstly, the safety of the technology, and secondly, the fear that the widespread practice of human cloning would undermine important social values and encourage eugenics or the manipulation of others as objects instead of persons. It is interesting that members of the Commission were aware of the speculative nature of these objections, and that a divergence of opinion existed within American society as to the appropriate values to appeal to in such a difficult and contentious area.

This stance, however, was a compromise, seeming to allow research as long as no cloned embryos were implanted in a woman's uterus. For some groups this resulted in two grave evils: the creation of a cloned human embryo, and its destruction in the laboratory. One spokesperson stated, 'This means it is OK to clone as long as you kill'; which brings us back to the embryo research debate, and even to the abortion debate. It is a perennial debate likely to continue for many years to come. It also indicates that the debate on any form of cloning utilizing human eggs and embryos will be closely allied to these more fundamental debates on the status one ascribes to the human embryo. Continuing debate in American political circles has strengthened this interpretation, with vigorous toing and froing between those intent on outlawing human embryo research, and their opponents advocating such research within careful constraints.

With the passage of time this distinction has solidified, as scientific societies have drawn very clear distinctions between the cloning of human beings, and cloning for *in vitro* research. Some, by advocating a moratorium on the cloning of human individuals, are attempting to comply with public outrage against such cloning. Simultaneously, they are attempting to leave the door open to laboratory research on cloning at a cellular level.

Some commentators recognized that what Dolly represented was a major scientific breakthrough, in that it answered important questions about the role of DNA as creatures develop into fully grown adults. However, at the same time it also makes it easier to alter the genetic make-up of animals, and brings closer the day when humans may be cloned. This is the correct order, both in terms of priority and importance – not the reverse. Nevertheless, there were those who also recognized the irony of our age, namely, that alongside scientific advances such as these there was an upsurge of unreason. And it was this unreason, with its credulity and ignorance, that may in part have been responsible for the apparent terror that cloning has evoked.

Calls for a moratorium on 'human cloning' were uttered far and wide, even though it was often far from self-evident what this term embraced. The Vatican issued a statement arguing that human beings have a right to be born in a human way, and not in a laboratory. It was said by some to attack the fundamental principle of human dignity, while there were concerns that it would allow third parties to biologically predetermine others. Perhaps more to the point was the reservation of David King, editor of *GenEthics News*, that cloning represents the tip of a relentless search for uniformity, efficiency and control, taking it into the realm of industrial efficiency. According to this critique, Dolly is a product of industry, and were this to be transferred to the human scene (even in a limited fashion) it would subject human reproduction to total direction and control. King writes

> In cloning a human being, the doctor would take total control of his or her genetic essence. Such a person would be a product of medical technology. The human input would be in the supply of raw material. As a technological product, the paramount consideration would be a precisely specified outcome. Am I alone in feeling that an

element of chance in our origins is essential to what it is to be human?[7]

Others were far more sanguine, with their awareness that it is what people actually do that is good or bad, not what they are capable of doing. Others were perplexed that people complain bitterly about the perceived threat of genetics to human dignity, but do nothing about grotesque insults to human dignity all around them. One scientist, the writer Richard Dawkins, expressed a desire to be cloned, since it would prove fascinating to watch a younger edition of himself growing up in the twenty-first century rather than the 1940s.

On a more serious (or should it be farcical) note, a physicist (not physician) by the name of Richard Seed, announced plans in early 1998 to clone a human being by setting up a cloning laboratory in Mexico. Despite the absurdity of this pronouncement (with its overtones of David Rorvik's *In His Image*), it made headlines and proved that human cloning needs no enemies when it has friends like Richard Seed. This was the sort of pronouncement aimed to bring every facet of the cloning enterprise into disrepute. Frighteningly, a project like this, with its dependence upon private funds, could have been carried out in the United States since it would have broken no law.

While the dominant reaction to the Dolly phenomenon was a mixture of repugnance and horror, a few lone voices started questioning what they saw as the hysteria of this reaction. While not rushing to advocate human cloning, they began to cast doubts on the rationality of the repugnance. Such people, including some scientists and ethicists, were far removed from Richard Seed. John Harris, for instance, a well-known British bioethicist, asked, 'Why not?' He considered that people were being driven by gut reactions and prejudices, and contended that the fact that things can be abused does not mean they will be abused. For him, people wanting to be cloned so that they could rear a child with

---

[7] D. King, 'Led by the Nose into Clone Cuckoo Land', 11.

the same genome as themselves would be bizarre. But, he said, a lot of parental motives are bizarre.

As we have already seen, Ian Wilmut has been solidly opposed to the cloning of human individuals (as against research using human embryos) all along. The use of cloning to replace a child in an accident would not produce the same person, nor would it bring back the child who had died. But it would be difficult to accept that the clone was a different person, and perhaps he or she would be expected to replicate the person being replaced. For Wilmut, these additional expectations would be unfair on the clone, and so to act in this way even for apparently exemplary reasons would be selfish and sad.

The current social and legal situation is, therefore, implacably opposed to human reproductive cloning, but with ambivalence in some quarters on human therapeutic cloning. For instance, the Human Fertilization and Embryology Authority (HFEA) in the UK will not issue a licence for any project that has reproductive cloning as its aim. On the other hand, it will consider licensing therapeutic cloning provided it falls within one of the purposes of the Human Fertilization and Embryology (HFE) Act of 1990.

I shall end this chapter with two comments. The first is to say that what Wilmut and team achieved was to uncover what might loosely be described as a new law of nature, since they demonstrated something exceedingly fundamental about how cells develop. Their achievement was far more profound than a mere technical trick. As one commentator put it, you can outlaw technique, but you cannot repeal biology. This is balanced by my second comment, that asexual reproduction is no panacea for our ills, and on a widespread scale it would be disastrous. Many years ago, a biologist, George C. Williams, likened it to xeroxing a lottery ticket. Even if you have the winning number, making copies will prove fruitless if the winning number varies each time.

Questions for group discussion

1. Much of the scientific work that has led to cloning was not concerned with cloning as an end in itself. This work is described in this chapter as 'not an example of spurious bravado or humanistic hubris, but scientific advances of quite a profound character'. Do you agree? What is the significance of this (if any) for social and theological discussions of cloning?
2. Discuss what you think of earlier speculations that cloning could increase the number of great thinkers, artists, athletes and beauties.
3. What do you think were Joseph Fletcher's and Paul Ramsey's major contributions to the cloning debate?
4. Should any of the cloning studies carried out at Roslin Institute have been stopped on ethical (or other) grounds?
5. How did you react to the announcement of the birth of Dolly? What were your reasons for this reaction?

Three

Beyond Dolly

In these initial chapters I am largely confining my attention to the cloning of individuals. This is human reproductive cloning. While I do not consider this to be the nub of the debate over cloning, I cannot avoid what are almost universal perceptions. Governments and political organizations do not pass resolutions banning a procedure without thinking they have very good reasons for doing so. For instance, Japan's parliament in late 2000 made the cloning of humans illegal and punishable by up to ten years in prison or a fine of US$90,000. By any standards these are sizable punishments. They also represent the first time in Japan that penalties have been imposed on a specific kind of research. Cloning is recognized by many as something apart from the common run of science, and it is the cloning of living, walking and talking human beings that is viewed as so horrendous. Some of these responses emerged in the previous chapter, and my task in the present one is to look a little more closely at what underlies these feelings. In the next chapter I shall pick up the issues surrounding the use of cloning for therapeutic purposes, so-called human therapeutic cloning.

Earlier debate on human reproductive cloning

In the late 1970s through to the mid-1980s, the ground was laid for what were to become some of the standard concerns and arguments regarding cloning. Inevitably, we are talking here about human reproductive cloning, because in those early days this was almost the only example of cloning that was discussed. This illustrates the limitations of ethical arguments in the absence of detailed science, since until society knows where a technique may lead, it lacks even the most fundamental sense of direction. This also illustrates the dangers of becoming caught in a time loop, where the ethicists and theologians are still discussing a particular procedure from a particular angle, failing to notice that the scientific community has moved on and is now confronting different issues and topics.

Concerns have surfaced repeatedly about cloning leading to alienation of our humanness. Over many years theologian Richard McCormick has questioned whether cloning will lead to a change in attitudes towards the meaning of our own humanness. Will it lead to a loss of respect for human life? In particular, if we manipulate and change very early embryos, will we gradually extend this to later embryos and fetuses? Others have carried this concern much further into postnatal human life. However, as noted earlier, we must remember that McCormick was discussing an extreme form of cloning which is not on most people's agenda today.

Paul Ramsey, whom we have already met, was an ardent opponent of human cloning in the late 1960s and early 1970s. As with other Christian thinkers of the time, his opposition was part of a deep ambivalence towards any manipulation of the reproductive process. His influential book *Fabricated Man* is filled with his concerns. For instance, the possibility of defects in any resulting children led him to his famous position that the only moral way to know the consequences of bringing an artificially conceived child into the world is by carrying out unethical experiments.

A blanket statement like this can only be justified if the dangers are substantial ones. To attempt to clone a child without a background of considerable animal research is surely unjustified – as it would be in practically every other area of medical science. But that does not seem to be the point Ramsey is making. For him, any form of artificial reproduction represents a transition of such magnitude that the first attempt would almost by definition be a step too far. Whatever the legitimacy of that position, its basis in likely harm is more difficult to justify. Previous animal experiments did not lead toward it, and a no-harm standard is to expect far more of an experiment than anything we routinely accept in ordinary childbirth or in routine surgical operations. Risks have to be taken, in ordinary life as well as in the laboratory. They are integral to every area of human activity, since life is full of risks and hence risks have to be accepted – as long as adequate safeguards are erected.

Cloning, albeit in the extreme version being discussed at the time, filled Ramsey with moral indignation. This arose from the assumption that knowledge of the genetic predisposition of clones might well prove to be psychologically and personally unendurable. He was appalled at the prospect of an elder teaching his or her 'infant copy', partly because of its strangeness and partly because of the problems that he thought would inevitably ensue.

More generally, Ramsey argued that those with a 'serious conscience' are prepared to raise ethical questions and conclude that there are some things that should never be done. By contrast, those with a 'frivolous conscience' raise ethical issues but then provide rationalizations for doing in the future whatever science makes possible. By its very nature, this argument condemns those coming at ethical issues from a background in science, since scientists are inclined to explore new territory rather than sit back and find reasons for not doing so. This does not justify pressing ahead with new endeavours, but I am not convinced that it inevitably means that scientists have frivolous consciences. One has to ask whether this distinction is a helpful one.

Leon Kass (*Towards a More Natural Science*), writing in the mid-1980s, was worried about whether the nature of humans themselves was being placed in jeopardy by artificial reproductive technologies, and especially by cloning. His antipathy to human inroads into reproduction has been expressed repeatedly over the years (including, as we shall see, very recently). In his famous essay 'Making babies', originally published in 1972, he expressed considerable alarm at what he witnessed occurring in reproductive laboratories. For him, any intrusion into reproduction was a violation, as the distinction between the natural and artificial became blurred.

> To lay one's hands on human generation is to take a major step toward making man himself simply another one of the man-made things. Thus, human nature becomes simply the last part of nature that is to succumb to the modern technological project, a project that has already turned all the rest of nature into raw material at human disposal, to be homogenized by our rationalized technique according to the artistic conventions of the day.

Kass's anti-technological stance becomes even more evident as he berates the intellectual and spiritual costs of seeing nature as 'mere material for our manipulation, exploitation, and transformation'. As humans themselves become the objects of technological intervention, Kass pessimistically views the erosion of our idea of a human being as 'something splendid or divine, as a creature with freedom and dignity'. Finally, there is the ultimate condemnation, that if we 'see ourselves as meat, then meat we shall become'.[1] Within this diatribe against scientific intrusion into anything human, cloning is inevitably cast as one of the worst of intrusions, especially cloning in a relatively eugenic guise.

Kass was unable to get away from the picture of a clone saddled with a genotype that had already lived. While he was aware that the environment would have an immense influence on the resulting individual, he was drawn to the thought that parents would manipulate the environment in an attempt to reproduce the person who had been copied. This was based on the premise that cloning would be carried out to reproduce some famous person and, therefore, the cloners would feel obliged to do all they could to see that this eventuated. This is what I have referred to as ego cloning, which until recently was almost universally pictured as the sole form of human reproductive cloning. For Kass, the conclusion was straightforward: the inevitable

---

[1] L. Kass, *Towards a More Natural Science*, 73–7.

stunting and warping of the child were enough to reject even the first attempts at human cloning.

Other concerns at the time were that splitting blastomeres may lessen respect for persons in general, and for the specific individuals who are cloned. It may deny them the individuality and uniqueness that reside in being a gift of nature. Taking another slant, some contended that splitting embryos is only possible when embryos and then children are regarded as interchangeable products: they would have to be regarded as material to be manipulated, just as in industrial processes, rather than unique individuals.

On the other hand, there were proponents of embryo splitting. Joseph Fletcher, whom we met in the previous chapter, was quoted twenty years later for his declaration that humans are epitomized by their making and designing abilities, and that the more deliberately contrived something is the more human it is. Others had little concern about a loss of genetic uniqueness, since the experience of twins does not lead us to sense any reduction in their sense of uniqueness and individuality. The pull and pressure of different environments, especially with twins (clones) living years apart, led some to conclude that they may not even recognize one another. Some writers, in countering the possibility that cloning may harm the clone, responded that the value of being alive outweighs any possible harms created by cloning. What they were saying is that, since the individuals in question would not have been born except by cloning, they have no cause for complaint. The alternative to coming into existence as a clone is not to exist at all, and these two states cannot be compared. This is not a satisfactory argument, since, if existence is always preferable to non-existence, it would justify any procedures leading to the creation of people. One cannot know precisely what will befall a cloned child, and the issue of non-existence or existence is probably misleading. Nevertheless, it does stress that every effort should be made to ensure that no harm befalls a cloned child once he or she is born.

It is fascinating to note that the argument against cloning, on the ground that the clone is identical to the original individual, had been dismissed in many quarters, since it is self-evident that the environment plays such a significant part in the moulding of the clone. A person's genome does not wholly determine their identity.

Social concerns about cloning were based on the premise that cloning would be indulged in en masse, and that it would rapidly become commonplace. Were this to occur, one might have scientific concerns about a decrease in genetic diversity, or social concerns about exploitation in the market place. Some envisaged there would be catalogues with pictures and information about cryopreserved duplicates being offered for sale. Hence, commodification and commercialism entered the picture. But why, we may ask, should this happen?

It is true that this has happened in the past with the slave trade, and unfortunately there is evidence that forms of slavery (including the sex slave trade) are in vogue today in some countries. But these have nothing to do with biological manipulation. All forms of slavery are tragic, but why would human cloning inevitably lead to commercialism and degradation of the human condition? As far as I can see, they are not inevitable, in that they only eventuate when we allow or encourage them to do so. If cloning were to be carried out to bring about these ends they would occur, but not otherwise. At present, even in the absence of cloning, there is nothing to stop them taking place whenever pressures exist for people to be used in these abhorrent ways.

The weakening of family and individual relationships was widely feared, leading to the concern that clones will be seen as objects to be used to serve parental purposes unrelated to their own well-being. What is important here are the motives for cloning. As one surveys this literature, it is difficult to escape the conclusion that much of the cloning discussion has been based on the assumption that the motives for cloning will be egotistical ones. Altruistic motives have not entered the picture, having been dismissed or not even contemplated. Altruistic motives may or may not be likely in this area, but simply to ignore them is misleading.

Another argument to appear in the 1970s was the right to ignorance on the part of the offspring regarding what he or she might become. What this says is that we are to respect the right of individuals to discover their own way and be a surprise to themselves. I have immense sympathy with this sentiment, since one can imagine an individual feeling a prisoner of his or her heritage: doing what has gone before, thinking what another has thought, reacting as another has done, having the same likes and dislikes as another. Were such a situation to arise, knowledge would indeed become a blighted chalice. But is this likely, seeing that cloned individuals would be vastly modified by their environmental experiences? I suspect that the extent of the ignorance enjoyed by a clone would depend on the expectations of the progenitors, and this brings us back to the reasons for cloning and our attitudes towards clones as human beings.

We also have to be exceedingly careful that we do not condemn biological cloning when we already indulge in what may be called 'behavioural cloning'. How often do parents expect their children to become doctors just like them, adopt the same political views as theirs, have the same religious (or anti-religious) beliefs as they have, and fit neatly into the same cultural niche as the one they occupy? Cloning of this type is well and truly alive, and we need to reject this at the same time as we attempt to outlaw biological cloning.

Why clone a child?

As we move to the present day, we continue to encounter a variety of views. However, there is now far greater openness towards accepting human cloning under certain well-defined circumstances. To some extent, this reflects the contemporary scientific perspective, allied with a less grandiose view of what cloning can accomplish in human society. Vistas directed towards producing an enlightened or superior race of beings, or alternatively, an army of drones, have largely disappeared. Were human reproductive cloning to occur, the possibilities envisaged now tend to be far more mundane. What we now encounter are:

- parents wishing to replace an aborted fetus, a dead baby or a child killed in an accident
- parents looking for a sibling to be a compatible tissue or organ donor for a child dying from leukemia or kidney failure
- a couple with a recessive lethal gene, who wish to have a genetically related child and, therefore, want to avoid the use of donor genes or selective abortion
- a family involved in a tragic accident, where the father has been killed and the only child is dying, and so the mother uses some cells from the dying infant to create a new child
- a wife whose husband is dying and who wishes to have biological offspring of the dying husband
- the desire of infertile or lesbian couples to have genetically related children
- an individual attempting to cheat death

These scenarios are, of course, hypothetical, but they serve to confront us with the whole gamut of possible reasons for carrying out human reproductive cloning. With the exception of the last one, each has a powerful therapeutic rationale, which is both its attraction and deception.

Attempting to cheat death is foolhardy and illusory, for the simple reason that the clone is a different person from his or her progenitor, who will die as inevitably as if he or she had not been cloned. We will live on in our clones as much or as little as we live on in our naturally conceived children. There is no way to cheat death, cloning or no cloning.

The use of cloning to provide a couple – heterosexual or homosexual – with a child does not involve imposing a particular plan on the child. The purpose is to have a child genetically related to one of the partners. This in no way justifies cloning in these instances, since there are crucial moral issues to be taken into account as well as the well-being of the child. Will the latter suffer psychological harm from being genetically related to just one of the parents? While it would be presumptuous to answer this categorically, there is ample evidence derived from children growing up with a step-parent, or following donor insemination

(DI), or where there is no genetic relationship to either parent as in adoption, to provide guidance. It is unlikely that the situation will be substantially different when the child has been cloned.

In the other scenarios, the children are being subjected to the special purposes or projects of adults. Each one prompts us to ask whether the child is being loved primarily for his or her usefulness, rather than for what they may bring to the world as unique individuals. The dangers in each case are immense, since each places the spotlight on the needs of an individual (parent, sibling) who is not the child to be born. The prospects of using the child to serve the purposes of another are extremely high, although not inevitable. It is easy to dismiss each of these scenarios as unethical and not worthy of serious consideration, and yet we are left with a nagging doubt. Perhaps cloning is not always as different as we might imagine from having children naturally. Nevertheless, the dangers are palpable, and one has to ask whether it is worth bringing cloning into the medical armamentarium for cases such as these. True, some of the cases are heart rending, but we all have to cope with suffering and loss, and a biological solution may be far more flawed and limited than we would like to think.

Another danger in some of these scenarios is to assume that the cloned child will be the same as the one so tragically lost. A replacement metaphor is gravely misleading. The parents would not be 'getting back' the same child that was lost; they would get a different child. The process is not the same as losing a toy and purchasing an identical one; children are not toys but human beings with all their individuality and newness, even if they have been cloned. Children are not interchangeable commodities, and no one should be encouraged to think they are.

An argument used by some in favour of cloning revolves around procreative autonomy, that is, it is for the woman to decide what she wants. If she wants a clone, she has the right to obtain one. If she wants a naturally fertilized child, that too is her right, as long as she can find a partner. And so it goes on, regardless of the partnerships or lack of them. I reject this since it ignores all moral constraints and boundaries. The woman's wishes override all else. In my view, this is moral anarchy, and has nothing to do with cloning per se.

Opposition to cloning: the debate today

Overview

Leon Kass has once again emerged as a strident opponent to human reproductive cloning. In his essay 'The wisdom of repugnance' he retraces steps already taken in his earlier essays on making babies. His criticism of cloning follows on from his critique of the artificial reproductive technologies. The nature of his critique is summed up with his description of Dolly as the work not of nature, nor of nature's God, but of a human, and of an Englishman at that. I have the suspicion that this places far too much stress on the manipulatory abilities of the English! In formulating his stance, he principally decries the most extreme and most self-centred forms of human cloning. This makes it difficult to assess the broader issues raised by cloning. His repugnance is such that rational argument becomes difficult. He writes, 'We are repelled by the prospect of cloning human beings not because of the strangeness or novelty of the undertaking, but because we intuit and feel, immediately and without argument, the violation of things that we rightfully hold dear. Repugnance ... revolts against the excesses of human willfulness, warning us not to transgress what is unspeakably profound.'[2] For Kass, cloning is a pollution and perversion of begetting; it is despotic, and a blatant violation of the parent–child relationship. It dehumanizes procreation, by degrading it through commodification. The difficulty with this is that arguments to back up these exceedingly strong assertions are hard to find. The emotional reaction shines through in his writings, but one gets the feeling that what he is describing is the most uncontrolled and unrestricted form of cloning imaginable. And yet, even in the midst of this diatribe, he

---

[2] L. Kass, 'The Wisdom of Repugnance', 20.

recognizes a possible place for at least some therapeutic cloning, as long as it is accompanied by a legislative ban on any form of human reproductive cloning.

How are we to respond to such strong denunciations as this? I do not believe we can seriously answer this question without considering what people like Kass mean by cloning. My reading of the literature leads me to suggest that they are talking almost exclusively about cloning on a mass scale and for the worst of motives. Like most other extreme scenarios this cannot be readily dismissed. This worst of all worlds scenario is feasible; it could come to pass. What we have to ask is whether it is inevitable.

I am labouring this point because it is no good rejecting something like human reproductive cloning on inadequate grounds. That is why in this section I shall assess each of the main objections to human cloning in a fairly critical manner. While I have no desire to support human reproductive cloning, rejection of it on inadequate grounds will backfire. As the inadequacy of the reasons becomes obvious, they will be discredited and cloning will quickly emerge into the public arena. After all, the doomsday predictions of thirty years ago regarding the artificial reproductive technologies had no influence on the scientific developments that subsequently took place in research laboratories. And why should they have done so, since they were describing a world that does not exist?

I deliberately devoted considerable space in the previous chapter to outlining the current state of the scientific developments, in order to provide a feel for the scientific driving forces at work. These will only be seriously directed by realistic policy discussions, not by employing scenarios far removed from what is likely to eventuate.

As one scans the literature criticizing cloning, it soon becomes evident that the arguments revolve around a limited number of themes. These are expressed in a variety of ways but they reflect common concerns. One expression of this is to say that cloning is a threat to human dignity, on the ground that an individual should never be thought of only as a means, but always as an end. Closely tied in with this threat is an undermining of individual uniqueness and unpredictability. In other words, it is seen as a threat on a number of counts, and I shall deal with each of these. However, we first need to ask a relatively simple question: how is the dignity of a natural twin threatened by the existence of a sister or brother? Does the existence of two very similar people tell us anything about their dignity? If it does, we have to think very carefully about the status of identical twins. If not, perhaps we are overplaying this particular argument against cloning.

Loss of individuality and autonomy

Diminished individuality is sometimes said to be an affront to human dignity, since there is no way of maintaining a clone's dignity if it can only walk in the footsteps of another. This could arise from a variety of causes: excessive demands placed on the clone by parents or genotype donors, expecting the clone to live up to a set of preconceived expectations, a closing of the clone's future because it is known what the progenitor is like. To force a clone to walk in another's footsteps would primarily be accomplished behaviourally rather than biologically.

I have already commented on behavioural cloning, where excessive demands are placed on individuals or groups to perform to certain expectations in, say, sporting, artistic or church circles. This is no more justifiable in these circles than it would be in cloning. We should have learned by now that even the most extreme efforts to turn genetic clones into human clones usually fail. With thirty identical twins born each day in the United States alone genetic sameness is a well-known phenomenon. The best-known and very tragic illustration of this was provided by the Dionne quintuplets, who were treated like identical circus performers when young. In spite of the way in which they had been homogenized throughout their childhood and adolescence, they all turned out differently. Such an aberrant upbringing strikes us with horror, but also proves how difficult it is to stamp out human individuality.

Along the same lines, there is an argument we have already encountered: the right to ignorance, to an open future, and to a quality of separateness. For writers like Hans Jonas, this is seen as necessary for the spontaneous, free and authentic construction of a life and self. I agree with this; what is more debatable is whether a later twin (clone) will know that his or her life has already been lived and played out by another. Will the later twin lose the spontaneity of authentically creating and becoming his or her own self? I have cast doubt on this because of what I predict will be the considerable differences between the two. I agree it would be tyrannical of the earlier twin (progenitor) to try to determine another's fate in this way. Hence, whether or not the later twin would always be haunted by the earlier one is speculative. In my view it is unlikely, given a healthy family and social environment. For instance, if you know that someone with an identical genetic constitution had failed in some endeavour (e.g. to run a marathon in under two and a half hours), you could learn from that and not bother with such an event or task – you could do something else at which you are better. In other words, you would have learned from the knowledge, rather than been limited by it.

The good news is that, in all probability, cloned children (just like ordinary children) will surprise us. And for that we should be exceedingly grateful. If left to themselves, they will probably demonstrate far more individuality than we could ever imagine. Of course, I may be wrong. I do not pretend to possess any infallible knowledge. But the doomsday merchants may also be wrong.

Let me reiterate. I am not arguing in favour of human reproductive cloning but am simply attempting to clear the ground. Would the individuality of clones be threatened by choosing for them their genetic identity? Does this amount to 'lording' it over them, in contrast to 'serving' them? I am not convinced the answer is an automatic 'yes'. It all depends on the motives and goals of the intrusion, just as it does now when conventional medical therapy is applied in young children to counteract genetic diseases.

Treated as objects

A related concern is that cloning will lead to an *instrumentalization* of human beings, where they are treated as objects and not as people. The concern here is that persons are being treated as things that can be exchanged, bought and sold in the market place. These are valid concerns, since the temptation to control the future direction of the child's life is very high. The more popular fear is that of mass cloning in a totalitarian society, where clones would be used as slaves. However, as I have pointed out already, slavery did not appear with the advent of cloning. Evil is not in the technique, but in the manner in which the technique is employed.

Care has to be exercised with this argument, since we repeatedly use people in occupations. When I send for a plumber what I expect from that human being are his abilities as a plumber. I am using his abilities, rather than appreciating him in his wholeness as a human being. No matter how good he is as a person, I will not be satisfied if he is an incompetent plumber. We do this repeatedly in economic life, and we all accept this as ethical as long as we realize that the plumber also has other attributes and the freedom to exercise those attributes under other circumstances. However, this is not always the case. Numerous parents make children instruments of their frustrated ambitions, their fantasies, or their desires for immortality. This does not mean to say that these children are used solely as instruments; some of them will also be loved. In practice, the balance between being used as instruments and being loved will vary from one extreme to the other.

What I hope is emerging is that to use another in this instrumentalized way may not be entirely bad, as long as they are paid for their services (in employment), and are accepted for what they are and loved for what they are (in the case of children). With children (conceived naturally or artificially), existence must be in the best interests of the child who must then be given freedom to develop as a new and unique individual.

Loss of genetic uniqueness

This has been a front runner in concerns over cloning for many years. But does our freedom depend upon genetic uncertainty, as if it somehow resides in the genetic lottery? Are we free as human beings only because of the unpredictability of our genetic combinations? Writing very shortly after the birth of Dolly, Axel Kahn stated in *Nature* that 'The uncertainty of the great lottery of heredity constitutes the principal protection against biological predetermination imposed by third parties, including parents.'[3] This is a theme that has appeared repeatedly in the human cloning literature, and genetic uniqueness is also a favourite argument used by Christian writers against cloning.

There seem to be two strands to this argument. The first is that the genetic mixing that occurs in sexual reproduction should not be meddled with by patients or doctors – they will simply alter it for their own ends and thereby impose upon the child a genetic combination of their choosing. This, it strikes me, is an argument more against genetic modification than against cloning, since the latter would be a very crude way of determining an offspring's genetic combination. Also, as we have seen elsewhere, this objection to cloning assumes that cloners will always have bad intentions.

The second strand is the more fundamental one: our uniqueness as individuals stems entirely from our uniqueness genetically. I have already made the obvious point that this does not apply to identical twins, who demonstrate unequivocally that whatever the relationship may be between human and genetic uniqueness, it is not a direct one. Let me explore this further.

Two people with identical genetic make-up will have different brains, which, of course, is what one finds with identical twins. This is because the organization of the brain is as much dependent upon soft wiring (influenced by the environment) as upon hard wiring (built in genetically). As the brain develops, the final form of its synaptic connections and networks depends as much

---

[3] A. Kahn, 'Clone Mammals ... Clone Man?', 119.

upon the environment as upon what is laid down genetically. The environmental influences are not mere afterthoughts or unimportant peripheral add-ons: the environment is essential for the final form of any brain. Change the environment, delay when sensory impulses arrive during development, and the resulting brain will be different from what it would have been under other conditions. This is why malnutrition, alcohol, and hormonal deficits during pregnancy can have devastating consequences for a child's subsequent intelligence and behaviour.

It does not take much imagination to realize that two individuals with identical genetic backgrounds will differ depending on what they see, who they interact with, the books they read, the films they see, the music they listen to. This is hardly surprising since one of the most characteristic features of the brain is its plasticity, the way in which it changes in response to the pressures both from inside and outside the body. Without this plasticity we would be unable to learn anything, memorize anything, respond to our world, or adapt to changing circumstances. All these facilities are essential for normal existence, and it is these same facilities which mean that genetic uniqueness is only part of the story for what makes us the unique people each of us are. The lack of genetic uniqueness by itself cannot be a threat to our freedom. To be that, it has to be overlain with other factors forcing us to conform to the whims of other people, who would have to force us to see what they want us to see, read what they want us to read, view the films they want us to view, listen to the music they want us to listen to, and so on and so on. It may be possible to manipulate someone's brain to be the sort of brain we want it to be, but that demands far more from behavioural pressures than from genetic ones.

What this is telling us is that genetic uniqueness and human uniqueness are far from being the same things. But then there is a final question: Is genetic uniqueness nearly as important as we often make out? If it is very important, why did God create a world in which it is possible to have identical twins? If we assume that identical twins are not aberrations, but perfectly normal people, we have to conclude that genetic uniqueness and genetic similarity are both ethically acceptable. There is a great deal of randomness in the world, and also a great deal of similarity, of which genetic similarity is one example. From a Christian perspective, both are inherent to the world God has created, and both must therefore be treated with considerable seriousness.

Additional issues

The risk of mental and physical impairment is frequently raised. This has come up previously and, as in any other area of scientific and clinical developments, it has to be taken seriously. There is no justification for proceeding with any procedure unless there is ample evidence to justify its use clinically, a pragmatic argument that applies here as in many other places. There is no difference between cloning and a surgical operation; if the chance of causing damage to the patient is unacceptably high, it is unethical to proceed. However, this is based on the assumption that those considering cloning may be driven by good motives, an assumption many writers reject, since for them cloning is always associated with unpalatable motives. That may or may not prove to be the case.

For some writers, cloning should not be indulged in since clones would be downgraded by society. There would be prejudice against them, and it is unethical to expose human beings to prejudice. However, any prejudice shown by society towards clones would be no different from prejudice towards any other minority group; all examples of prejudice are to be decried and efforts are to be directed towards removing or preventing them. The demands placed on clones will probably be closely aligned with the reasons for undertaking the cloning in the first place. There is a potential problem here, but cloning is not unique in this regard.

Theological arguments against cloning

Many of the writers I have alluded to up until now have been
writing from a Christian perspective, and yet the arguments have
not been explicitly Christian or even in many instances explicitly
religious. However, as we shall see, Christian writers also refer to
issues such as human dominion, and the contrast between begetting and making.

Impersonal element

John S. Grabowski, a moral theologian from the Catholic University of America, finds three major reasons against human
reproductive cloning: (1) it oversteps the limits of human dominion; (2) it violates human dignity; and (3) it reduces its products
to subpersonal status. His concern is that cloning amounts to
making human beings (as opposed to begetting them), so that we
stamp them with an inferior and ultimately subpersonal designa-
tion. While he admits that a clone would not be identical to the
original person, he sees in cloning an attempt to produce a
genetic replica of a human individual, something that strikes at
the heart of the irreducibility that constitutes personhood. The
dignity of the person is, therefore, violated. In his view cloning
removes the personal relations of parenthood (just like other
artificial reproductive technologies) and substitutes the impersonal ones of producer and product. A clone has no parents, only
an original; hence its origin is entirely impersonal. For him, the
origin of human life is torn from the bodily gift of a man and
woman to each other in love and reduced to a laboratory procedure – this is an unworthy beginning for a human person and
oversteps the bounds of legitimate human dominion. This in his
estimation serves to foster a culture of death. For him cloning
reduces humans to chattels, reminding us of the slave trade and
of Nazi eugenics.

Grabowski's critique of cloning centres on the impersonal
aspects to the process, and hence the dignity of the person is
threatened. However, the impersonal (or subpersonal) emphasis

is overdone, since it is difficult to see how a clone's origin is entirely impersonal when he or she is derived from a person. Even if one disagrees with the procedure, the way in which humans are subsequently treated is not automatic. At present, we do not treat humans as chattels if they were conceived by rape or incest or in a culturally unacceptable liaison. Christians, in particular, should deplore any such possibility, and should be vigorously opposed to human clones being treated in subpersonal ways.

Donald Bruce, Director of the Society, Religion and Technology Project of the Church of Scotland, comes out against human cloning on the grounds of the *uniqueness* of humans. For him 'to replicate any human being technologically is a fundamentally instrumental act towards two unique individuals – the one from whom the clone is taken, and the other the clone itself'.[4] This he regards as unacceptable abuse, something that should be outlawed worldwide as a crime against humanity. I have already dealt with these arguments, and so shall not repeat myself here.

Abigail Rian Evans from Princeton Theological Seminary has no doubt that human cloning is morally wrong. The reasons are as follows: it is not a necessary solution to any human tragedy; it fosters a *reductionistic* rather than a holistic view of human nature, treating people as means not ends; it undermines the structure of the family and human community; it creates a pressure to use this technology and make it a god. She considers that these reasons are grounded in Christian theology. In her view cloning should be banned, since it fails to meet the criteria of glorifying God, recognizing God's sovereignty, honouring each person's dignity, and practising stewardship of the earth.

While I remain to be convinced by some of these points, her emphasis on the dangers of reductionism is worth heeding. I shall return to this in a later chapter. Human beings are more than their genes, and the desire for a genetically related child is not the most fundamental of all desires (even though it is an important consideration for many couples). Cloning, therefore, should not

---

[4] D. Bruce, 'A View from Edinburgh', 9.

be resorted to in isolation of other considerations, and should only be considered in the most extreme of circumstances (if this ever becomes feasible). Evans is correct in pointing to the pressure this technique would create within societies. Nevertheless, it would be helpful to know how her emphases stem from a recognition of God's sovereignty. These and other theological aspects need to be explored.

Making not begetting

In speaking as a Protestant theologian Gilbert Meilaender reminds us (in his article 'Begetting and cloning') of the creation story in Genesis, with its connection between the differentiation of the sexes and the begetting of a child. For him maintaining the connection between procreation and the sexual relationship of a man and woman is essential both for that relationship and for any offspring. The male–female relationship is seen by him as foundational, since once this is lost the sexual act and any resulting children become the province of individuals and not of a couple. Hence he sympathizes with those who see cloning as *narcissistic* and as nothing more than a replication of one's own self. To him the whole process is demeaning, reflecting one person's own desires.

This points to a fundamental issue, namely, the relationship between the artificial reproductive technologies in general and cloning. Part of Meilander's rejection of cloning is also a rejection of the all artificial reproductive technologies. Any technical intrusion into human procreation can be seen as threatening the personal relationship between male and female, whether this is AIH (artificial insemination by husband), IVF (or one of its many offshoots) or cloning. What we have to ask is whether these objections are inherently biblical. There is no doubt that each technique can be misused or even abused, but this by itself is not an argument against their very existence.

Meilaender also draws a distinction between begetting and making. While 'begetting' results in someone like us, 'making' results in someone unlike us. Begetting expresses equal dignity, since we are not at each other's disposal; whereas making loses this sense of equality. These criticisms of course apply to most of the artificial reproductive technologies, although cloning is viewed by Meilaender as a new and decisive turn down this road. From this perspective, cloning is even more a form of production, 'far less a surrender to the mystery of the genetic lottery … far more an understanding of the child as a product of human will'.[5]

Two issues emerge. Firstly, will the resulting children actually be viewed as a product rather than a gift? This is a pragmatic argument, and empirical evidence should be available on the basis of what we know about IVF and DI children. I see no evidence to support this contention. For example, an extensive study was carried out by Robert Snowden and colleagues in the early 1980s on couples who had received DI over a forty-year period. While this study concentrated on issues surrounding the couples, such as the reasons for undertaking DI, the secrecy involved, and the effects on the social father, it also emerged that in most cases the children had been willingly accepted into the family. Only a few children could be included in the study, but these were pleased to feel that their parents had wanted a child so badly that they had gone to the length of resorting to DI; they were also pleased to be that child who had fulfilled their parents' wishes. The father–child relationship did not seem to have been damaged in these instances by the knowledge that DI had been utilized. In a later series of studies by Susan Golombok and colleagues on family relationships where children had been conceived using IVF and DI, the results showed that the quality of parenting in families with a child conceived by assisted conception is superior to that shown by families with a naturally conceived child. No differences were found for the presence of psychological harm in the children or for children's perceptions of the quality of family relationships. Inevitably, there will be additional dimensions if cloning is the means of bringing the child into existence, and these will have to be assessed at that

---

[5] G. Meilaender, 'Begetting and Cloning', 43.

time. However, the feedback from DI children suggests that the consequences will not generally be nearly as catastrophic as sometimes painted.

The second issue to emerge from Meilaender's stance is that of the genetic lottery. This is an instructive term, since it points to the unknown nature and the uncontrollability of biological processes. This forces us to ask whether the lottery element of genetic inheritance is integral to God's plan for human reproduction, and the extent to which such an inheritance may be controlled.

The randomness of genetic inheritance is basic to sexual reproduction with the redistribution of characteristics that go to make up the emerging individual. Consequently, any process that had major repercussions for this redistribution would be foolhardy, since it would take us well beyond human abilities – now and perhaps at any time in the future. But does this also mean that the occasional deviation would be catastrophic? The answer appears to be 'no' since identical twins are deviations with which people cope remarkably easily. While intentional cloning introduces many other considerations (as we have seen), the genetic issues raised by cloning are not dissimilar to those encountered with identical twins. Cloning on a vast scale would have detrimental consequences genetically, but this would probably not be the case if it were to be on a very limited scale.

What about the stress placed by Meilander on human will? Why should we look to mystery rather than understanding? When the gene lottery goes seriously wrong, resulting in distressing diseases, we attempt to rectify what has gone wrong. True, this is done indirectly, by manipulating the results of the genetic errors. But is there any difference *in principle* between this and directly influencing genetic combinations? I do not want to take this argument further here, since it gets us into gene therapy rather than cloning. The issue at stake is not the detail, but the extent to which we are prepared to accept what the genetic lottery turns up. To accept whatever it doles out is genetic fatalism, and a rejection of the wholeness of human existence. To glory in such determinism is a strange irony for Christian thinkers.

Human dominion

Cloning can be condemned because it exceeds the limits of the delegated *dominion* given to the human race by God. It has been argued that cloning inevitably involves this, since humans were not given the authority to alter their nature or the manner in which they come into existence. Cloning, therefore, is akin to eating the fruit from the forbidden tree in the Garden of Eden, that is, the tree of the knowledge of good and evil. One has to accept that this is a possible interpretation, but by the same token it has to be questioned why altering some aspect of our nature is doing this. And is cloning so different from the many medical procedures and illustrations of control that are not condemned in this manner? Along these lines it is sometimes inferred that the biological nature of every person is untouchable, and therefore by definition beyond the reach of scientific investigation. Once again, though, this tends to be applied selectively; prenatal existence is untouchable, postnatal existence is not untouchable. But why this distinction? If it is always untouchable, every routine medical procedure becomes unacceptable.

At this point two biblical images, Eden and Babel, may be of general usefulness in framing a Christian perspective. In Eden the human creature is given dominion over the garden with responsibility to till and keep it (Gen. 1:26; 2:15). The dominion is limited, since it does not extend to the Pleiades and Orion (Amos 5:8) or to the mountain goats, hawks, the crocodile or hippopotamus (Job 39 – 41). The world was not created by us or for us; we are to enjoy it, and we are to develop it judiciously as stewards. That is one side of the picture. The other side is provided by Babel (Gen. 11), where we are confronted by ambition and the desire to be like God. In terms of this picture, the role of steward has been overlooked, and everything is trampled underfoot, to control and master for the sake of mastery. When this is combined with the power afforded by modern technology, chaos looms.

Both pictures apply to humans with their God-like abilities, and we have to take both seriously because our abilities can be harnessed for good uses, or they can be wielded for destructive ones. Neither tells us to sit back and do nothing; each is a reminder of what we are to do but also where we can go wrong. Their power lies in their general sense of direction. They will not tell us whether it is appropriate to go in the direction of human cloning, or whether we should stand back and totally reject cloning. They will not provide categorical directions, because as human beings we have to decide how to use our abilities and choose the paths along which we are to travel.

Objections to animal cloning

The General Assembly of the Church of Scotland resolved in 1997 to 'Commend the principle of the production of proteins of therapeutic value in the milk of genetically modified sheep and other farm animals, but oppose ... the application of animal cloning as a routine procedure in meat and milk production, as an unacceptable commodification of animals.'[6]

Donald Bruce warns against adopting an unfettered view of human progress and improvement, since he sees this as not being consonant with a view of the human condition in which human finiteness and fallibility are essential ingredients. Restraint is needed, which for him means that human beings should do their best to maintain the variety of God's creation. This allows him to approve of some animal cloning, where there are obvious bene-fits for humans but where the animal problems are few. He argues that the main intention of any such cloning should not be cloning as such but producing animals of known genetic composition.

This is an interesting position, although it may be difficult to work out in practice. The Church of Scotland has come out

---

[6] Church of Scotland, *Cloning Animals and Humans.*

against cloning in routine animal production in all cases where natural methods have been side-stepped simply on the grounds of economics or convenience. The fear here is that the mass-production principles of the factory are being brought too far into the animal kingdom: as God's creatures, animals have freedoms that should be preserved. From this it is a short step to reject any procedure that bows down to the demands of consumerism. For instance, the highly efficient control of animals from birth to death is regarded by Bruce as treating animals far too much like a device or an instrument, such as a widget.

For those who object to the use of animals in medical research, cloning represents a further step down an ethically unacceptable path. Animals are being viewed in both reductionist and commercial terms; they are being exposed to harm, and this approach is a spiritually impoverished one. These criticisms bear striking similarities to those put forward against human reproductive cloning, and their strength depends upon one's view of animals in relation to humans. There is little doubt that great care and restraint should be exercised in the treatment of animals when employed for human ends, but this alone does not argue against the use of all animal cloning procedures.

Alternative theological perspectives

Theological arguments do not lead inevitably to a complete rejection of human cloning. The rejection of cloning on the ground that it destroys the uniqueness of human life does not convince some theologians, like Ted Peters. Even if clones were to have identical genotypes, the two individuals concerned would have different phenotypes (just like identical twins), a different sense of self, different thought processes, and different ethical responsibility. Their biological uniqueness would remain, let alone their spiritual uniqueness. For Peters, individuals' uniqueness also lies in their relation to God, something that is not determined by DNA; it depends on God's active grace, and on God's desire to love us. Our value or dignity relies upon our alien dignity, bestowed by God and independent of our genetic status. Peters comments that our identities in society come from growing into society, while our identities before God come from his ongoing grace and from our desire, or lack of it, to live in close communion with him.

Peters is also unimpressed with the distinction sometimes made between identical twins and clones, in that twins arise by chance, whereas clones result from human intention. This is an argument against human choice in determining genotype. He contends that this argument presupposes that what nature bequeaths prior to human choice has a higher moral status than what happens when we influence nature through technological intervention. But why should genetic predetermination by human decision-making make cloning immoral when twins exist naturally? Should they be prevented from coming into existence?

Peters is not arguing in favour of cloning; rather, he is objecting to what he sees as bad arguments. Like others, he is concerned about the cloning of humans, mainly because the practice may commodify children as a result of economic pressures. His worry is that it may lead to us thinking of children as products, as the outcome of technological reproduction with quality control standards. He wants to sound warning sirens, while not advocating a total ban on human cloning. Peters is prepared for a world of expanded choice, and he wants to construct an ethical vision to take account of this. Such a vision would treat children with dignity even when they are the product of advanced reproductive technology or, as he phrases it, the gift of this technology, since God loves them as much as he loves us.

Ronald Cole-Turner is suspicious of the argument that cloning violates the natural order of sexual reproduction. While recognizing that children may have a distinct advantage by having two genetic parents, he is not prepared to place weight on a natural order of the family. This argument has been repeatedly misused in the past to justify racism, unchecked competitiveness, genocide and war. He does not think we know how to find moral guidance in nature. For him

Christians find their best clue about nature by looking at Jesus Christ, where we see nature rightly related to God and where we see its destiny prefigured in Christ's resurrection. In Jesus Christ, we see a welcoming of children that transcends genetic parentage. From this we might infer that cloning is a matter of indifference. It may not be something Christians will choose ... but it is not something they will try to prohibit.[7]

Creation as a completed act

But can we go further? The Christian writers adamantly opposed to cloning tend to view creation as a completed act. The natural world as we know it reflects the world created by God, and it is a given. This suggests that humans are not to tamper with God's good creation, nor with the make-up of humans themselves. Put simply, God's likeness cannot be improved upon. Consequently, human nature must not be modified in any way, particularly the biological component of our nature. Our biological nature is a given; the way of bringing humans into the world is a given; the organization of our bodies and brains is a given. The givenness in each of these instances suggests that boundaries have been placed around them, boundaries that are not to be transgressed.

Bible illustrations that might be used in favour of this interpretation are references to boundaries that were not to be crossed, any crossing of them being forbidden: eating the forbidden fruit; sex between humans and animals (Lev. 18:22–4; 20:12, 15–16); cross-breeding animals, and planting a field with different types of seed (Lev. 19:19; Deut. 22:9); constructing a garment of both linen and wool (Lev. 19:19; Deut. 22:12). On this basis, cloning can be condemned since it would transgress the dimensions of sexual reproduction as created by God.

It is true that boundaries were set in these instances, but it is not self-evident that these boundaries provide infallible guidance to cloning. Why were these boundaries erected, what was the rationale behind them, and is this relevant when we think about

---

[7] R. Cole-Turner, 'At the Beginning', 128.

human cloning? What is it about cloning that demands it should be outlawed from the moral community? The Old Testament boundaries were intensely practical ones, and we have to ask whether this also applies to human cloning. As we have seen, there are practical considerations, and they have to be examined very closely. Nevertheless, they appear to be a long way from stating that we are eating the fruit of the tree of genetic knowledge, an act akin to eating the forbidden fruit. Provocative as this is, it requires justification before it can be taken seriously. By all means let us erect boundaries, but we have to exercise considerable wisdom in deciding what the boundaries are, and where they are to be placed.

Viewing creation as a completed act leads to an acceptance of the world as we know it, and yet few would push this interpretation too far. It features prominently in the genetic and prenatal areas, but is largely ignored in other biomedical areas. More usefully, it leads to an emphasis on therapy as opposed to enhancement, that is, rectifying disease and that which has gone wrong, as opposed to attempting to improve upon that which has been given. This is a useful guide in most situations where disease is the focus. But where does cloning fit in? Would cloning be an example of therapy or enhancement? In my view, it is closer to therapy than to enhancement.

Creation as a transformative process

Christians who espouse this approach interpret the beginning of Genesis as: 'When God began creating the heavens and the earth …' Creation, within this interpretation, was not a completed act but was a transformative process. God moved the world from a chaotic nothingness to an ordered light-filled, life-bearing place. God improved what existed. When we view his creation in this manner, what lies at the heart of it are God's good purposes and not a particular form of creation.

From this it follows that humans might have a role to play as creators; after all, our creation in God's image emphasizes our creativity and inventiveness. When we act as stewards of God's creation, we put our creativity to work to assist the remainder of creation. Hence, our God-ordained creativity is not some sterile, abstract ability of little practical relevance; it is to be employed in major endeavours: to overcome disease, alleviate poverty and hunger, expand the wealth of human achievement, and develop technology across many broad fronts.

As we move along these paths, we continually have to ask ourselves where the line between continuity and transformation is to be drawn. If creation is a transformative process and if we have a part to play in bettering our world, our assessment of human cloning will depend on whether we use human cloning to do good or evil – the motives and end result are crucial, not the cloning itself.

Seeing God's hand in the uncertain and mysterious is relatively easy, whereas seeing his hand in what we can control may be difficult. Cloning and genetic engineering offer the prospect of removing that randomness and uncertainty; but would this undermine the belief that humans are created by God in his image? It depends on what we take this to mean. In the final analysis, we are left with the wonder of creation and the gift of new life, regardless of how it is actually brought into existence. And surely it is the gift that is significant rather than the means employed, as long as the means are ethical and worthy of our status as beings in God's image?

Alongside this consideration we can place another: the less one's sense of identity is based on the physical, the less threatening cloning becomes. We are more than just our bodies, no matter how central our bodies are for our sense of identity. Why, then, should we be lesser people because there are copies of us in existence?

The transformative view also confronts us with the query of whether we can change the world for the better. When it comes to eradicating diseases the answer has to be in the affirmative. As beings created in the image of God, we are creative just like God. We go on changing the world and ourselves; in a sense we create a new world. On the other hand, we should rightly be concerned that our creativity can be used unwisely and that it can lead us astray. We make unwise decisions and unwise choices, and we act selfishly and do things for our own interests, opposing the interests of others. So often our powers are simply inadequate and limited; we do not know what is for the best, and we cannot look far enough or accurately enough into the future.

These queries serve to remind us that we need to exercise enormous caution as we transform the world. It is no light task, and whenever undertaken in isolation from God we do it at our peril. The givenness of our world and our ability to transform it are both limited pointers to how we act in the biomedical arena, and more precisely how we face up to the possibility of human reproductive cloning. Unthinking acceptance of cloning, just like unthinking rejection, will be found wanting. We must walk a middle path, seeking to transform what needs to be transformed but gratefully accepting much else as given. Guidelines will be found in what is good for human beings and what will best serve them and their lives in community with other human beings.

Where are we now?

What conclusions have I arrived at in the light of the issues raised in this and the preceding chapter?

1. Human reproductive cloning is not to be encouraged, since the temptation to make other people in one's own image is too great, as is the danger that cloning of this type would almost inevitably be too closely linked with commercial drives. While I do not regard this technology as inherently evil, its widespread use would create pressures difficult to resist. I am not in favour of attempting to outlaw it, since I am not convinced this would be either justified or effective. The challenge is to decide whether any of the reasons put forward in its favour (e.g. infertility) are strong enough to allow its very limited introduction. I shall attempt to paint a far broader picture within which to assess these possibilities in the remaining chapters.

2. Cloning is frequently viewed as the worst possible d   ment that could confront the human race. It is a great   that so little attention is paid to the ways in which the gene   potential of humans born into impoverished environments   today is stunted and thwarted. Why do we so resolutely   ignore the good we could do by committing adequate   resources to alleviate malnutrition, providing adequate clean   water supplies to numerous populations, and ridding coun-   tries of killer diseases like malaria? Equitable health-care   systems would save countless lives each day, and yet some-   thing as relatively untechnological as this is overlooked. Is it   really true to say that the existence of human clones is worse   than countless children dying needlessly each day from pre-   ventable diseases? This is not an argument in favour of   cloning; it is simply attempting to place it in perspective.

3. For many, 'human cloning is a moral and emotional minefield   that should place it among taboos such as cannibalism or   incest'. This comment, from a 1998 editorial in *Nature*,[8] is a   call to quiet reflection on where we are heading. It places the   prospect of human cloning into a wider social context, where   the aspirations of scientists have to be balanced against the   fears and deep concerns of many others. By the same token,   neither should we become so engrossed in hair-splitting   debates on some features of exceedingly early embryos that   we overlook the possibilities for medical advance that lie   around the corner.

4. Were human clones ever to exist they would be normal   human beings; they would not be freaks; they would know as   much of God's grace as anyone else; and they would have an   alien dignity bestowed upon them by God. Societies would   have to ensure as far as they were able to that human clones   would be treated as people in their own right, having an open   future. They should never be created to satisfy the whims or   desires of other people, or be viewed as products. Idealistic as

---

[8] *Nature*, 'Hubris, Benefits and Minefields of Human Cloning', 211.

the latter sentiments are, they apply as much in a world without clones. Tragically, they are repeatedly ignored.

5. For Christians, extremely pressing issues are raised by this debate: the role of control in biomedical procedures; the role of genetic uniqueness in assessing what constitutes a person and personal freedom; the requirement to think issues through in very detailed terms since vague general statements are no longer adequate in these biomedical areas. In other words, what should be realized is that there is no substitute for good arguments in assessing possibilities like cloning. This stands out when looking at human reproductive cloning, but we shall return to it again when confronted by the vistas opened up by human therapeutic cloning and stem cell research.

6. In the final analysis we have to be people of character who work to produce societies of character, since in the end our motives and intentions are crucial. While this is of very general applicability, we come face to face with it in a poignant way when the prospect of producing human clones is on the horizon.

Questions for group discussion

1. What do you see as the major reasons against human reproductive cloning?
2. Can you foresee any situation in which you would resort to human reproductive cloning?
3. If you had the opportunity of (1) banning human reproductive cloning, or (2) eliminating malaria from the world, which would you do, assuming that only one were possible?
4. If you were a clone, how do you think you would respond to the person who had had you cloned (that is, your 'father' or 'mother')?
5. What theological arguments for or against human reproductive cloning do you find most convincing?

6. To what extent do you think creation is a completed act? How much do human beings attempt to alter their worlds? How much should they?

Four

Beyond Reproductive Cloning

Up to this point I have concentrated on human reproductive cloning. However, I think it is of limited value to discuss this form of cloning as though it were an isolated technology. It should have become obvious that this is far from the case. Ian Wilmut, in particular, has made it very clear that the interests of his group were not in cloning for its own sake. They were not trying to make some megalomaniac statement about the power of scientists, nor trying to demonstrate the way in which power-hungry scientists in white coats can manipulate human beings. Nothing could have been further from the truth. Instead, they were intent on solving some basic problems in developmental biology, and in seeing to what extent cloning and genetic manipulation can be developed for use in the pharmaceutical industry (see Chapter 2).

These explorations may or may not be welcomed throughout the community, and of course they have to be analysed on their own merits. But they are a far cry from a world in which cloning is sought after as a means of changing human society. The science underlying the developments referred to in this book has nothing to do with agendas aimed at improving human beings.

Cloning fits into quite a different agenda, that of genetics and the dilemmas associated with genetic developments and genetic control. In my book *Valuing People* I dealt with various issues in this realm, including gene therapy, enhancement genetic engineering, the significance of genetic screening for the setting of insurance premiums, and the contentious issue of patenting human genes. I also examined what might be meant in the genetic area by notions such as playing God, tinkering with nature, and going down a slippery slope. And I touched on the ambiguity of genetic knowledge. Although such issues are relevant in a cloning context, I shall not repeat here what I wrote in my earlier book.

In this chapter I shall return to fundamental issues in developmental biology, and to the other form of cloning I have touched on in previous chapters: human therapeutic cloning as opposed to human reproductive cloning. The goal of therapeutic cloning is to produce tissues for use in medicine rather than for the production of new people. While therapeutic cloning is an entity in itself, it will probably be used in close association with other techniques, chief among which is the use of stem cells to produce new cell lines and tissues.

It will also be of value to deal briefly with the Human Genome Project (HGP), since this opens up further avenues for fundamental advances in biomedicine. The HGP has nothing directly to do with any form of cloning, but it provides an important part of the current climate for discussion of biomedical manipulations. What these techniques have in common is their immense power to be used in medical treatment, sometimes in ways that will appear dramatically different from anything with which we are currently conversant.

Human therapeutic cloning

Human therapeutic cloning refers to the use of somatic cell nuclear transfer (SCNT) to produce tissues rather than complete individuals. The way this would work would be to take the nucleus from an ordinary human body cell (almost any cell will do), and insert it into a donor egg which has already had its own nucleus removed. This would result in the production of an embryo, even though fertilization has not occurred; indeed, sperm have been omitted altogether from the process. Embryos produced in this way can go on to develop normally to adulthood; Dolly is a prime example of this. However, by halting the growth of the embryo at five to six days, embryonic stem cells (see following sections) could be extracted and grown in the laboratory. In theory, these stem cells could be coaxed into forming any tissue type in the human body.

Therapeutic cloning has not attracted nearly as much bad press as its more infamous counterpart, human reproductive cloning. Despite the relative lack of attention from the media, therapeutic cloning is infinitely more important than the cloning of individuals. This is because the production of tissues and cell lines has momentous potential for the treatment of injury and disease. The beauty of this approach is that tissues developed from stem cells, themselves derived from 'cloned' embryos, would probably be largely free from rejection since they would be genetically compatible with the individual from whom the donor nucleus was taken, that is, the individual being treated. It is not known at present whether the situation would be as clear-cut as this in practice, since the cytoplasm of the donor and cloned tissue is different (that is, the mitochondrial DNA contained in the cytoplasm of the enucleated egg differs from that used in the nuclear replacement process).

I have attempted to distinguish clearly between therapeutic cloning and reproductive cloning. Nevertheless, the very term 'cloning' carries a stigma for many, who are inclined automatically to reject therapeutic cloning regardless of any differences between the two forms of cloning. This may be a reason why some authorities now use the term somatic cell nuclear transfer (SCNT) rather than therapeutic cloning. The mythology of cloning and the deep repugnance of many at the cloning of individuals has carried over into the cloning of tissues, which is regrettable.

In the eyes of some writers, human therapeutic cloning (regardless of its name) is to be likened to preying on unborn human embryos. As we shall see when we come to stem cell technology, opposition to it centres on what can or cannot be done to human embryos. Any form of biotechnology stands or falls on these grounds. C. Ben Mitchell, Senior Fellow at The Center for

Bioethics and Human Dignity in Illinois, considers that we should acknowledge the dignity of human beings and refuse to cannibalize those who are least able to defend themselves.

A more nuanced approach is that of Donald Bruce of the Church of Scotland's Society, Religion and Technology Project. His opposition to human therapeutic cloning is based on the following: First, it is illogical to create a cloned human embryo knowing that it will have to be destroyed on ethical grounds (because it is unethical to allow it to go to term). Second, he is concerned that were cloned embryos to be created, the pressures would be too great to stop going to the next step and implanting them in a woman's uterus. Third, he considers that human therapeutic cloning would necessitate treating human embryos instrumentally, reducing them to being nothing more than a resource from which convenient parts are taken. Fourth, this procedure would remove any vestiges of a special status for the human embryo, while any reprogramming of embryos would mark a profound ethical change to what is considered right about the embryo. For Bruce, reprogramming would convert the status of the embryo into that of a ball of cells. He also has concerns about growing organs in the wake of therapeutic cloning, since a holistic view of the human person might find this repulsive.

Opposition to this form of cloning can well be appreciated, but what does it tell us about the cloning itself? Fertilization has not taken place, and so the status of the resulting organism has to be ascertained. I shall look at this in the next chapter, where it will become obvious that we are walking a tightrope between the familiar and the unfamiliar. There is no doubt that we are delving into uncharted territory, where conventional concepts may or may not hold. We will have to ask whether the contrast is indeed that between a human embryo made in God's image, on the one hand, and a ball of cells on the other.

Since human therapeutic cloning is so closely bound up with stem cell technology, I shall make further comments on ethical issues raised by human therapeutic cloning after I have dealt with this other form of technology.

Stem cells

Just a few years ago, hardly anyone outside developmental biology had heard of stem cells, simply because they had no relevance either for ordinary people or for everyday medicine. All that is about to change very dramatically. Before we look at the developments and the possibilities, we need to explain what stem cells are and why they might be very important in the future.

In simplest terms, a stem cell is an unspecialized cell at an early stage of development. Naturally, therefore, they are present in large numbers during the early stages of an individual's development when tissues and organs are being produced. From them, specialized cells like liver cells, kidney cells, and nerve cells are produced. During development, many stem cells are capable of giving rise to a wide variety of different cell types. However, once development has come to an end, the need for stem cells decreases considerably, so that in adults their role is limited to renewing certain selected tissues throughout an individual's life. For example, they constantly regenerate the lining of the gut, they revitalize skin, and they produce a whole range of blood cells.

This is one side of the coin. The other is that adult cell types, like muscle cells, cannot revert to being stem cells. That is, specialized cells cannot retrace their steps to become unspecialized or undifferentiated. In other words, the movement from unspecialized to specialized cells and tissues is one way. This, at least, has been the accepted dictum until very recently. All this is now beginning to change as the potential of stem cells is being realized and as vistas are opening up for obtaining stem cells from adult tissues.

Confusion frequently arises over the different terms used to describe stem cells: multipotent stem cells, pluripotent stem cells, and even totipotent cells. *Multipotent stem cells* can be derived from fetuses, and are present throughout life in some organs, although their numbers decrease with increasing age. These stem cells are thought to be able to give rise only to a specific type of cell, for example, neural stem cells can give rise only to nerve cells. *Pluripotent stem cells* are derived from embryos and are known as embryonic stem (ES) cells. It is these stem cells that feature predominantly in discussions of stem cell technology, since they have the potential to give rise to any cells of the body. Their potential usefulness is, therefore, huge. More specifically, they are derived from the blastocyst, which is an early stage in embryonic development. In addition to these embryonic stem cells, there are also embryonic germ (EG) cells, which are derived from the fetus – from regions destined to develop into sperm or eggs (primordial germ cells). Both ES and EG cells are examples of pluripotent stem cells, and it is the potentially unique versatility of these ES and EG cells that presents enormous scientific and therapeutic promise. The third term sometimes used is that of *totipotent cells*. Unfortunately, there is confusion over these: on some occasions they are equated with pluripotent stem cells, whereas on others the term refers to cells that can develop into an entire organism. When used like this, they are only found at the two- to four-cell stage of embryonic development.

With these definitions in mind, let me return to more general issues. Stem cells can be obtained from the following sources:

- human fetal tissue following elective abortion (EG cells)
- umbilical cord blood
- human embryos created by IVF and no longer needed by the couples being treated for infertility using IVF (ES cells)
- human embryos created by IVF for research purposes, to provide research material (ES cells)
- human embryos generated by SCNT or other cloning techniques (ES cells); this source involving the reprogramming of adult cells is no more than a theoretical possibility at present; it could include the use of hybrid embryos

Regardless of which source is utilized, stem cells can be grown in the laboratory, and they can be coaxed to differentiate into cells and tissues, such as skin, bone, cartilage and blood. The excitement and potential accompanying this technology is immense, as a large range of diseases becomes amenable to treatment. Organs damaged by disease or injury could be repaired, notably following: heart attacks and heart failure (with heart muscle cells), diabetes (with insulin-producing cells), osteoarthritis (with cartilage cells), hepatitis and cirrhosis (with liver cells), and osteoporosis (with bone cells). Blood cells could alleviate conditions ranging from cancer to leukaemia, and nerve cells could benefit a range of central nervous system conditions like Alzheimer's and Parkinson's diseases, multiple sclerosis and spinal cord damage.

Although this description has been in terms of future possibilities, some limited uses of stem cells have been available for years. For example, they have been successfully isolated from adult cells in bone marrow, skin and blood, and have been used in the treatment of leukaemia and some gene disorders. On the whole, however, the majority of these stem cells have only had the potential to develop into the type of tissue from which they were isolated.

As already mentioned, stem cells are present in aborted fetuses and umbilical cord blood of newborn babies. Relatively little is known about the potential of these sources, and it may be that these stem cells only have the capacity to develop into specific tissues. For instance, those from cord blood may be limited to producing bone marrow and blood cells. In the latter part of 1998 a research team hypothesized that primordial germ cells, which are the precursors to egg and sperm cells, should be undifferentiated at the very early stages of development. Embryonic germ (EG) cells were derived from human fetuses at five to nine weeks of age (aborted for therapeutic reasons), when undifferentiated cells are migrating to the developing ovaries and testes. When grown on a specific 'feeder' layer of mouse fibroblasts (which secrete factors that inhibit differentiation), EG cells have properties that parallel those of embryonic stem cells (see below). Both sets of stem cells display pluripotency.

While cord blood will pose few ethical problems for most people, the same cannot be said for the use of aborted fetuses, where the same issues will arise as in the grafting of brain tissue from aborted fetuses into patients with Parkinson's disease. For a discussion of these issues see my book *Valuing People*.

Embryonic stem cells

Scientifically, embryonic stem (ES) cells currently appear to possess the greatest potential, in that they can probably develop into a wide range of tissues, whether heart muscle, bone marrow or nervous tissue. For this reason they are described as pluripotent. Stem cells are grown from early embryos in the laboratory, a procedure that has already shown considerable promise in mice. Mouse ES cells have been utilized in vast amounts of research, including work on embryogenesis, gene function and the modelling of human disease.

Until recently, difficulties in isolating and culturing these cells have meant that researchers were unable to establish and maintain similar human cell lines. However, very limited work of this type has now taken place using human tissue. In this, embryonic stem cells have to be taken at five to six days after fertilization from the inner cell mass of the blastocyst (at which stage the blastocyst consists of 150–200 cells).

In the latter part of 1998, two sets of researchers simultaneously but separately, isolated and cultured human embryonic stem cells (HES). One group, headed by James Thomson, derived the cells from the inner cell mass of blastocysts acquired from spare embryos donated to co-operating IVF clinics. This work was confirmed in April 2000, when human embryonic stem cells were isolated from four blastocysts, and when it was additionally demonstrated that stem cells can be frozen for storage and grown again once thawed. It was also demonstrated on that occasion that neural stem cells can be isolated and persuaded to form mature nerve cells.

One of the attractions of stem cells is that it may be possible to create tissue banks of these cells (and tissues) for transplantation. Such banks could be created for individuals in case of subsequent illness (one assumes this would only be done where there were known compelling factors to do so), and they may be combined with SCNT techniques.

What will stem cells enable us to do?

The potential of these new cells is profound. As mentioned previously, any disorder involving loss of normal cells could be a candidate for replacement therapy, with the prospect of bringing immense relief to patients. Although it is unlikely that replacement organs will become available in the foreseeable future, one can speculate that banks of graft tissue could be generated for blood, bone marrow, lung, liver, kidney, tendons, ligaments, muscle, skin, bone, teeth, retina and lens. There have already been successful examples of the culturing of mouse ES cells to form *in vitro* colonies of nerve cells, skeletal muscle and vascular endothelial cells. Besides these, human ES cells could also be used to generate tissues for the pharmaceutical testing of new drugs and toxicological agents. They also have the ability to improve our understanding of the complex events that occur during normal human development, with a view to understanding what goes wrong to cause diseases and conditions such as birth defects and cancer.

It is all too easy to concentrate on what may become available and the benefits this may bring, and overlook what is required to get from where we are now to where we could be in five or ten years' time. The gap between the two is where research comes into the picture, and it is frequently the research stage that forces us to confront ethical issues. It is as if we look forward to the finished meal, but want to ignore everything involved in actually preparing that meal. Stem cell therapy is currently in an early phase of the research stage, since the scientific and technical hurdles that need to be overcome will require a considerable number of years of basic research. Fundamental issues in cell and developmental biology remain to be solved. For instance, what initiates and maintains the processes of differentiation? What determines the cell type(s) into which any particular stem cell will differentiate? To answer questions like these requires a great deal of research on both animal and human cells and embryos. While the bedrock of this research is provided by animal experiments, detailed queries regarding human applications can only be answered on human tissue. This is a general principle in all areas of human therapy. It is not, of course, inevitable, since society and individuals may decide to reject the use of stem cells in human research, and to turn away from any possible medical benefits for human populations.

The problem here is that it is very difficult, if not impossible, to predict in advance which research projects will prove of benefit, or what direction any particular research project will take. This is why scientists are very wary of allowing politicians and policymakers to determine which are the best research projects to pursue. Numerous dramatic advances have stemmed from very unlikely projects, using very unlikely experimental models. Who would have suspected that major advances in our understanding of brain mechanisms would have come from the study of snail nervous systems, or huge advances in cancer therapy from work in genetics?

And so, when we contemplate advances in stem cell research, the best we can do is to follow useful leads across a broad range of possible sources of stem cells. This is why, from the scientific perspective, it appears that stem cells from both fertilized and cloned human embryos will have to be explored at some point, both from a scientific angle and with technical and safety considerations in mind. This does not mean to say that embryonic stem cells will remain the most desirable source of stem cells, simply that they will probably have to be used for experimental purposes during developmental stages of the research.

Such statements do not advocate these approaches; they are simply put forward to show what is required if work in this direction is to continue. By all means reject the final goal – possible medical therapy in this instance – but do not accept that goal and reject the only way we know of arriving at it.

Ethical issues raised by stem cell research

The ethical controversy surrounding the utilization of stem cells in humans opens once again the related debates about elective abortion, and the use of human embryos for research. In other

words, it precipitates a re-examination of these morally con-
tested questions at the beginning of human life. However, it also
reminds us that these are far from theoretical questions, since
what depends upon them is the possibility of improving human
welfare through increasingly powerful and precise technology,
and the limits set by important ethical obligations.

The ethical issues addressed by official bodies within countries like the UK and the United States are built upon those
already elaborated in connection with other forms of research on
human embryos. This is well illustrated by the UK Department
of Health report, *Stem Cell Research: Medical Progress with
Responsibility*, published in 2000.

The premises on which the recommendations in this report are
based are that stem cell technology will usher in considerable
potential benefits for human health; research using cells or tissues
from adults does not raise insurmountable ethical problems; the
use of fetal tissue in therapy (such as fetal tissue grafts in patients
suffering from Parkinson's disease) has been ethically approved.
Nevertheless, the report concedes that the use of embryonic stem
cells is contentious, and therefore it has to be determined whether
the use of embryos in this manner represents an unjustified extension of current uses to which embryos are put.

Currently, any use of embryos in the UK must comply with the
1990 UK Human Fertilization and Embryology Act. This Act
and a report from the Warnock Committee have laid out the following principles for the use of embryos in research:

- the human embryo has a special status, but this is not the same
  as that of a living child or adult
- the human embryo is entitled to respect beyond that accorded
  to an embryo of other species
- such respect is not absolute, but should be weighed against the
  benefits arising from the proposed research
- the human embryo should be afforded some legal protection

Under the Human Fertilization and Embryology Act research
using human embryos is permitted in the UK up to fourteen days'

gestation, provided the research is related to reproductive questions and embryonic development, having the goal of improving infertility treatment and contraceptive techniques, and in general benefiting future embryos. More specifically, the main purposes are to promote advances in infertility treatment; increase knowledge about the causes of congenital disease; increase knowledge about the causes of miscarriage; develop more effective techniques of contraception; and develop methods for detecting the presence of gene or chromosome abnormalities in embryos prior to implantation.

The 2000 Department of Health Report followed the earlier guidelines and legislation and accepted that human embryos can be used instrumentally, in that the embryos will not themselves receive any benefit, since this is an inevitable outcome for all spare embryos no longer required for treatment. It also accepted that the research purposes should be broadened, since the general medical benefits anticipated from stem cell technology could not have been envisaged in 1990. The 'balancing' approach put forward by the Report weighs embryonic ethical considerations against any significant potential health benefits expected to accrue for many other groups in the population.

Similar conclusions were reached, again in 2000, by the Nuffield Council on Bioethics (*Stem Cell Therapy: The Ethical Issues*), which concluded that there are no grounds for making a moral distinction between research into diagnostic methods or reproduction, and research into far more general potential therapies.

In both reports, the move from embryo research with reproductive goals in mind to research of general medical interest is accepted. The Nuffield Council report argues against a moral distinction between these two, since there is no qualitative difference between them; and while neither benefits the embryo in question both may benefit people in the future. Each form of research involves using the embryo as a means to an end, and since one form of research is accepted so should the other. The use of donated embryos is accepted, since the alternative is allowing them to perish. Rather than denoting lack of respect for embryos, this should be viewed as analogous to tissue donation.

The Nuffield Council report finds no compelling reasons to allow embryos to be created (via IVF) merely to increase the number of embryos available for ES cell research or therapy. This emanates from concerns about the commodification of human embryos, using them as a means to an end, and hence lowering the respect owed to the embryos.

In accepting the use of fetal tissue for the derivation of EG cells, the Nuffield Council starts from a basis previously elaborated for the transplantation of fetal material (following induced abortion) into patients, say, with Parkinson's disease. The basic ethical (and procedural) principle had been laid down in 1989 by the Polkinghorne Committee, according to which any decisions regarding the abortion, and then the subsequent use of tissue from the aborted fetuses, have to be completely separate. The aim of this is to ensure that no woman can become pregnant with the intention of having a subsequent abortion in order to donate tissue from that fetus to someone known to her. No matter how noble such an intention, it would mean that the fetus was being created in order to serve the interests of someone else. For most people that is unethical. The Nuffield Council recommended that any use of EG cells should follow these same lines. Inevitably, those who oppose abortion and who also see an indissoluble link between the abortion and any subsequent use of fetal material, will be unconvinced by any of these provisos.

Additional ethical issues raised by human therapeutic cloning

Since human therapeutic cloning does not involve the creation of genetically identical individuals, it appears to circumvent the ethical minefield surrounding human reproductive cloning. However, therapeutic cloning will normally make use of early human embryos, precluding its acceptance by those who do not approve of the manipulation of human embryos under any circumstances.

The first crucial concern here is that human therapeutic cloning would deliberately *create* embryos solely for research (or possibly therapeutic) purposes. Currently, the majority of embryos used in research are spare embryos left over after IVF treatment. The second issue is the adequacy of the supply of human eggs (oocytes).

The 2000 report from the Department of Health accepts that embryos may be created by cell nuclear replacement. This technique could potentially be used to create compatible tissues or organs from stem cells for transplantation, or to investigate mechanisms for reprogramming adult cells. An understanding of how adult cells might be reprogrammed to behave like unspecialized stem cells, could also provide compatible tissues for repair purposes. In arriving at this decision, the report took considerable care to emphasize that such research should only be permitted if there was no other means available of obtaining this sort of important information. In line with existing UK legislation, the report rejected the possibility of implanting embryos created in this way into a woman's uterus. An amendment to the 1990 Human Fertilization and Embryology Act was passed by the UK Parliament towards the end of 2000, as a first step towards allowing the cloning of human embryos for the extraction of stem cells. The House of Lords approved the new regulations in early 2001, raising the possibility of human stem cell trials in the UK by as early as 2004.

The Nuffield Council report accepts that research on human embryos derived in this manner will be essential for the safe development of stem cell technology. The justification for this is provided by the significant potential medical benefits expected to come from such research. This is an entirely pragmatic and consequentialist argument, but would that automatically invalidate it if use of the technology had been preceded by adequate research on cells in culture and by animal experiments? The hope of the writers of the report is that this research will eventually permit researchers to reprogram the nuclei of somatic cells in such a way that the resulting cells differentiate directly into stem cells, thereby bypassing the need for a source of oocytes and the development of an embryo. The question one has to ask here is whether this hope is a realistic one, and whether, if one disagrees with the work proposed, the long-term goals outweigh any short-term disadvantages. If the immediate work is considered unethical (and perhaps even evil), it may well be that future positive prospects will not be considered sufficient to outweigh the short-term evil consequences.

Reactions to stem cell technology

As one surveys the general responses to the developments in stem cell technology, there is little if any opposition to the use of stem cells from adult tissues. In these instances, the likely beneficial effects for medicine are welcomed. Enormous store is placed by reports coming out of laboratories for the treatment of cancers, autoimmune diseases, anaemia, stroke, and corneal scarring. However, quite a different response is frequently encountered to the possibility of using embryonic stem cells, derived from early human embryos (or embryonic germ cells from aborted fetuses). Here the antagonism to destroying human embryos, or using them either for research or for therapeutic purposes, takes over. This, in turn, leads to an emphasis on the value of adult stem cells in clinical work. Although the ability to treat or heal those who are suffering is seen as a great good, it is claimed that not all methods of achieving a desired good are morally justifiable.

A number of reasons are given for opposing embryonic stem cell technology. The first is that it uses material considered to be derived from morally illicit sources, since one group of vulnerable human beings is being sacrificed for the benefit of other human beings. This is considered to be discrimination, because human embryos are viewed as a weak, under-represented group (they are the tiniest of human beings), that is being singled out for destruction. Second, we turn human life into a mere object if we create and destroy innocent life for our own ends. This emanates from what is sometimes called unbridled utilitarian notions, and is regarded by some as part of a culture of death.

Third, members of the human species (human embryos) who cannot give informed consent for research are being made into experimental subjects, even though they personally will not benefit from the experiments. Fourth, research into embryonic stem cells is looked upon as tainting all stem cell treatments. Fifth, the thinking behind this research is claimed to be the same as that which led to Nazi experimentation in the 1930s and 1940s, and as the US Government radiation experiments during the Cold War. Sixth, lurking behind the scenes is the quest for immortality, and the desire to ward off aging itself.

These arguments are of two varieties: ethical and scientific. The ethical takes us directly to our view of the human embryo at its earliest stages of development, while the scientific stands or falls on its own merits. Of these two, the ethical is given greatest prominence in public debate on stem cell research. For instance, in the United States, the Center for Bioethics and Human Dignity has argued very strongly in this way, as has the National Conference of Catholic Bishops. These and similar-minded organizations encourage people to oppose any research in which human embryos are destroyed principally for the above reasons. However, another strand of thinking also appears in the arguments, namely, that research of this nature is unnecessary, since new and dramatic breakthroughs are taking place using adult stem cells (bone marrow from adults and fetuses, and neural stem cells from living human nerve tissue and adult cadavers). The argument here is that these adult sources are equally, or even more, promising than embryonic sources. This may or may not prove to be correct.

The first four reasons against embryonic stem cell research revolve around the status of the human embryo. For some this source can never be justified, and that is the end of the story. However, it is also noticeable that this blanket prohibition is bolstered by additional reasons for rejecting the research: the creation of embryos solely for research purposes, the inability of embryos to give informed consent, and their use to benefit others (non-embryos). This medley of reasons frequently has a Christian basis, which is perfectly understandable, since one would expect a Christian perspective to enlighten the broad compass of the debate. Nevertheless, one has to be careful in specifying precisely the sort of contribution one expects the biblical writers to bring to the debate on stem cell technology, as it is self-evident that they can make no direct contribution to the details of the debate. What, then, is their contribution thought to be?

Those Christians who are deeply opposed to the use of embryonic stem cells are opposed to the destruction of human embryos. In other words, it is this that they are opposing rather than stem cell technology per se. Hence, any stem cell research that utilizes human embryos is seen as downgrading the high value that should be placed on the unborn, on the assumption that the unborn are human beings who are created, known and uniquely valued by God. This viewpoint is based on biblical passages such as Job 31:15; Psalm 139:13–16; Isaiah 49:1; Jeremiah 1:5; Galatians 1:15; and Ephesians 1:3–4. This stance is further supported by Genesis 9:6 with its warning against the killing of fellow human beings, who are created in the image of God. Human embryonic life is also said to exist primarily for God's own pleasure and purpose, and not for our purposes (Col. 1:16). Any use of human embryos in stem cell research is viewed as sacrificing one class of human beings (embryos) to benefit another (those suffering from serious illness). Additionally, we must not do evil that good may result (Rom. 3:8).

This position has to be taken very seriously by Christians. While the end result is not specifically Christian, in that many others adopt the same position, its intention is exemplary, namely, the protection of human embryos. I have enormous sympathy with this stance, although, as I have stated in other books (*Manufacturing Humans* and *Valuing People*), a simple absolute position may be unattainable. For me, we should aim to place very considerable value on human life at every stage – the early embryo, the later embryo, the fetus, the infant, the child, the young adult, in midlife, and in old age. Serious ethical questions have to be addressed at each of these stages, and in the early embryonic context one is: should human embryonic life ever be sacrificed for research or therapeutic purposes?

Any approach to this question has to incorporate a number of components. What is the stage of development of the embryos (say twenty-four hours, four days, fourteen days, or eight weeks)? Are the embryos by-products of IVF procedures, that is, spare embryos left over from attempts to produce children? What is the fate of these embryos if they are not used for research purposes? Alternatively, have they been produced specifically for research purposes? What are the prospects of the research making major contributions to human welfare?

These questions will be regarded as irrelevant and a distraction by those for whom no research on human embryos can ever be justified, and it is not my intention to take this matter any further at this point. I shall return to it in the next chapter, when I look more closely at the moral status of the blastocyst. All I want to state here is that the absolute position is not the only one that can be adopted by Christians. The biblical passages referred to above point clearly towards the moral commitment we should display towards any prenatal human life. However, our moral commitment towards all human life is equally clearly spelled out by one biblical writer after another, and we dare not divorce the one from the other. Any research that may be carried out on human embryos should be circumscribed, otherwise we will soon find ourselves using embryonic life for our own (questionable) ends. Similarly, the creation of embryos for the sole purpose of using them as research subjects would appear to be unacceptable. Obviously, the biblical writers did not state this (how could they have done so?), but the tenor of protection for the unborn seems to point in this direction.

The ancillary reasons for combating stem cell research are less convincing. The argument based on the lack of informed consent by embryos themselves is a non-argument. After all, no embryos, fetuses or young infants can provide any informed consent for any procedure carried out on them. The ethical question is whether procedures not in their immediate interests should be carried out on them. No matter how we answer this, the issue of informed consent will be of little assistance. Similarly, with the quest for immortality; any medical advance can be interpreted in this light. Consequently, any or all medical advances can be condemned for this reason; it should be dismissed as a red herring.

The intrusion of the Nazis into this debate is to be expected, but does it help? What it does is highlight widespread mistrust of scientists and their endeavours. The Nazi experimentation on humans was an unmitigated evil. The differences between that and what we are discussing here should be obvious for all to see, even for those who oppose embryonic stem cell research. Guidelines are in place, regardless of their acceptability or otherwise to societies at large, and very serious ethical discussions are actively taking place – the scientists proposing to experiment on human embryos do not have Nazi-like intentions.

The value of assessing the arguments against embryonic stem cell research is to highlight current attitudes and sensibilities, since these cannot be ignored. There is no doubt it would be preferable to use non-contentious adult tissue wherever this is possible, since any ethically debatable approach will be surrounded by practical problems in most societies, even when there is considerable agreement that it should proceed. Neither scientists nor clinicians generally wish to become entangled in bureaucratic webs if these can be avoided. It is also true that both the social and scientific contexts are moving rapidly. For instance, towards the end of 2000 a report of the twelve-member European Group on Ethics in Science and New Technologies came out against the creation of human embryos for use in stem cell research. According to this, the creation of embryos for the sole purpose of research raises serious concerns since it represents a further step in the instrumentalization of human life. Such a stance has to be taken seriously.

At the same time, an increasing number of reports are appearing in the literature showing that adult tissues could prove to be a more promising source of stem cells than previously thought. There have recently been reports of blood stem cells generating muscle tissue and muscle stem cells generating blood cells. Brain cells can be regenerated, leading to the speculation that all types of brain cells might be regenerated from an adult stem cell. This is not reality at present, and it may not turn out to be this simple. Regardless of the pros and cons of any position in the scientific area, the status of all the science is rudimentary, and is changing very rapidly. All approaches are experimental and much work still needs to be done before any of them will enter the therapeutic arena. Hence, we need to be very cautious in drawing hard conclusions prematurely.

What emerges from the ethical and scientific approaches is that each should be able to benefit from the other. Scientists should not be allowed to run rampant; indeed, they should not wish to do so. The ethical concerns provide a bridge to society's legitimate concerns about the rights of human embryos; they are also giving science an opportunity to explore alternative approaches. On the other hand, ethical concerns should be soundly based on the status of the contemporary science, with its continually emerging new insights and directions.

Michael Nazir-Ali succinctly summarizes the issues: 'Scientists do not have all the answers. Neither do theologians, philosophers or ethicists. In this most tricky of areas, we all have a responsibility to find the moral way forward – and we need continual dialogue on what will do the least harm and promote the greatest amount of good.'[1]

The Human Genome Project

So much I have been dealing with has been exceptionally contentious. However, as we turn to the Human Genome Project (HGP) everything seems to be different. One has only to listen to the welter of public pronouncements to get the clearest feel imaginable for this. At the time of the announcement of the completion of the draft map in mid-2000, grandiose claims were made by politician and scientist alike: 'Today we are learning the language in which God created life'; 'We have caught the first glimpses of our instruction book, previously known only to God'; 'For the

---

[1] M. Nazir-Ali, 'A Growing Concern for us All', 4.

first time we've rolled back the big stone and peered into the sepulchre with our tiny flashlights, reading the sacred script off the tablet.'

It is amazing how biblical metaphors come into their own in the face of scientific developments like this. We saw the same at the time of the cloning announcement. The very magnitude of the achievement, its grandiose dimensions, its uncertainty and scope all appear to take us into mystical and religious territory. On this occasion, however, the responses were positive rather than negative. But why should the HGP be regarded in such a positive light while reproductive cloning is seen so negatively? The prospects for manipulation of the genome will probably be greater as the repercussions of the HGP unfold, and yet it is cloning that is associated with such terrifying prospects.

Knowledge of the human genome will redefine knowledge of ourselves. This is its power and its potential. The leaders of the two sequencing groups (Francis Collins and Craig Venter) recognized this and the work remaining to be done, with their references to the many tasks lying ahead before we can 'speak the language of the genome fluently', and to the genome sequence 'representing a new starting point for science and medicine'.

The aim of the HGP is to analyse and sequence all the DNA on all the human chromosomes. The project was initiated in 1990 as an ongoing fifteen-year program (although it will have been completed much quicker than this). Simple as this appears, it brings biology into the realm of 'big science', both in terms of the worldwide effort required and the costs involved. The project is characterized by collaboration between bodies such as the National Institutes of Health (NIH) and the European Union, loosely held together by an international group of scientists called the Human Genome Organization.

Running neck and neck with the Human Genome Organization in the sequencing race has been a privately funded company, Celera Genomics. Concerns have been expressed in some quarters over the involvement of Celera Genomics, which has not accepted any public money and is therefore under no obligation to make its data public. In contrast it has always been the Human

Genome Organization's intention to ensure that all sequence data is freely available and in the public domain. This, they hope, will encourage research coordination and collaboration, and ultimately maximize the benefits to society.

Despite the often acrimonious competition between the two rivals throughout the project, they reconciled their differences for the joint announcement of the draft map of the human genome in June 2000. Prior to this, the inaugural results of the HGP appeared in the form of the first complete sequence of a human chromosome, number 22. Chromosome 22 is one of the smallest of the chromosomes, but is nonetheless thought to be gene-rich. At least 27 human disorders are believed to be associated with this chromosome, including cancers, trisomy 22 (the second most common cause of miscarriage) and schizophrenia. Following on from this milestone, the complete sequence of chromosome 21 was released in May 2000.

By all estimates, a complete and end-to-end copy of the human genome will be available by June 2003, two years ahead of schedule. In order to understand the immensity of the accomplishment it is necessary to take a brief look at the science behind the project. The substance of the genome is deoxyribonucleic acid (DNA), which is a code made up of four letters (or bases), A, C, G and T. The human genome comprises approximately three thousand million letters, in endless variations. It is this sequence of letters that the HGP is attempting to decode, and to determine where the genes lie among the jumble. This task is made even more difficult by the fact that more than 95 per cent of the letters in the genome represent so-called junk DNA, with no apparent purpose. Our genes are described as being scattered throughout the genome like stars in the galaxy, and it is incredibly tricky to separate out the genes from the junk. The initial sequencing of a rough draft of the human genome was published in February 2001 by the Human Genome Organization and Celera Genomics. There are around 30,000 human genes.

As if the mapping of the human genome is not time consuming enough, the HGP is also very interested in the genomes of other species, or so-called model organisms. At the genetic level, all species are surprisingly similar to each other, and comparisons of human DNA with the DNA of model organisms can make the human sequence much easier to understand, and may aid in locating disease-causing genes. To date, the other organisms fully sequenced include yeast, bacteria, a roundworm, and a fruit fly. The decoding of the mouse genome is also well under way, and the zebra fish and the rat are waiting in line.

The benefits to medicine from the HGP

The primary goal of the HGP was, and still is, to improve human health. The mapping of the human genome is likely to revolutionize the practice of medicine. It offers the promise of improving our lives and health through uncovering the genetic triggers for many diseases; not just for single-gene disorders but also for the host of more common complex diseases such as diabetes, heart disease, schizophrenia, and cancer. Differences in susceptibility to many of these diseases result from human genetic variation. It turns out that our differences stem from an alteration in approximately one genetic letter per every thousand. These seemingly insignificant differences are known as single nucleotide polymorphisms (SNPs). An SNP database is envisioned, allowing researchers to compare specific genetic variations between diseased and healthy subjects. Studies of this nature on SNPs have considerable potential since they could help to identify genes which contribute to complex but common diseases, genes which have, thus far, been remarkably difficult to track down.

Once this is done, exquisitely sensitive diagnostic tests can be devised, which make diagnosis of disease sure and treatment swift. Analysis of the human genome may yield genes that are promising drug targets, allowing the development of more effective drugs. The advent of 'personalized medicine' is also envisaged, where treatment and preventative programs are tailored to an individual's genetic profile. This makes use of the relatively new field of pharmacogenomics, which is the matching of drugs to individuals on the basis of their genetic profile. This is particularly useful since some drugs might help one patient but cause dangerous side-effects in another. Armed with this increased knowledge doctors will then prescribe a personal regimen of immunization and screening, in addition to lifestyle measures, to prevent the most likely diseases throughout an individual's life. These huge strides forward in our understanding of biology and the genetics of disease are likely to translate into a change in emphasis from diagnosis and treatment, to prevention.

However, such optimism must be tempered. We may know the bulk of our complete genetic code, but we may not understand the meaning, or the 'translation', of that code for many years to come. It has been estimated that it will take most of this century to analyse all of the information. Also, knowing the code for a gene is not the same as knowing what protein it produces in the body, or what that protein does, or what happens when something goes wrong with that particular protein. This sort of information transports us into the realm of proteomics, the latest trend in the post-genomic era. The ultimate goal of proteomics is the cataloguing and analysis of every protein in the human body, a project as enormous in magnitude as the mapping of the human genome. Nevertheless, a number of biotechnology firms including Celera Genomics have taken up the challenge with the launching of proteomic programs.

Molecular medicine has been in existence as a branch of medicine for some years, its thrust being an understanding of disease based on genetics (hence the adjective 'molecular'). However, to date, molecular medicine has made only very small differences to treatment; it has not as yet revolutionized medicine. The potential may be there, but the reality has been disappointing. The HGP should accelerate the contributions of this area very considerably indeed, but caution is in order.

Ethical concerns with the HGP

The HGP raises a great number of ethical questions. From the moment of its inception, the HGP recognized its responsibility to address the broader societal implications of the new-found knowledge. In order to accomplish this, the project commits 5 per cent of its annual budget to a program that specifically addresses the ethical, legal and societal implications of genome research (the ELSI program). This program has focused on a number of high priority areas that include privacy and fairness in the use and interpretation of genetic information, issues surrounding genetics research, and public and professional education.

Issues of privacy and confidentiality have always permeated health care, but the availability of genetic information raises unique and pressing concerns. For example, in some cases genetic information about an individual will also provide information about family members. Who is, or is not, entitled to this information? Will it be used to discriminate against individuals by insurance companies, potential employers, courts, or schools? In the near future something as insignificant as a sample of saliva could be used to test for an individual's predisposition to any number of diseases. In the light of the huge potential for misuse of genetic data, genetic privacy warrants special attention. Some countries have attempted to address this through the development of specific policies and practices designed to protect confidentiality in genetics research. The majority of these relate to discrimination by insurance companies or employers, but unfortunately, many of these have yet to be taken up, or are weakly enforced.

Fairness in the use of genetic technologies is another major concern. Who will have access to these expensive technologies, and who will pay for their use? On a larger scale, what percentage of research budgets should be devoted to this project? How much should be spent on identifying and treating genetic diseases, as opposed to other conditions that cause disease, such as poverty, drug and alcohol addiction, poor housing and education, and inadequate access to reasonable primary health care?

Another priority area is public and professional education regarding the new technologies stemming from the HGP. Genetic testing and genetic counselling, and their associated ethical, legal and social implications, will impact greatly on current health care practices and health care professionals. Many physicians are poorly trained in genetics, and yet they will be asked to be proficient genetic counsellors in the future. Health care professionals are not the only ones lacking the relevant understanding. The public too will need educating about the future impact that genetics will have on their lives.

There are many other pressing ethical issues surrounding the implications of the HGP, such as that of eugenics. There is likely to be a percentage of the population who would like to use genetics to 'improve' the human species. Research of this kind should ideally be limited to therapeutic improvement, with the curing of diseases brought about by genetic abnormalities. However, where does one draw the line? The distinction between a 'disease' and a 'trait' becomes blurred when one considers such things as obesity or hyperactivity in children. This is the difficult debate, not whether it might be used to improve intelligence or produce blue-eyed babies. So much of the debate surrounds the latter but ignores the former, and yet it is the former that sits at the boundary between normality and abnormality, health and disease. Similarly, the boundary between therapy and enhancement is blurred, not clear-cut. This is where the ethical dilemma resides.

The HGP also has the potential to alter the way we think about ourselves. The reductionism that is entailed by the HGP could conceivably have a number of consequences. First, knowledge gained from the HGP may lead to the construction of a 'standard' human genome. If this occurs, one must then ask what variation society would view as permissible before an individual's genome was labelled as substandard or abnormal? This is not substantially different from the standard charts we are all familiar with; one has to decide how flexible the standard is and how it is to be interpreted. Genetics is no different from any other measure, and we must not think it is.

Second, claims of the discovery of genes associated with various behavioural characteristics such as a propensity to violence or criminality, to suicide, or risk-seeking behaviour could lead to our actions being viewed as 'genetically determined' and inevitable, rather than a matter of free will. Such claims suggest that there is a deterministic one-to-one relationship between a gene and a behavioural characteristic. This is inaccurate and unhelpful, since the few reports of this nature remain unconfirmed, and much scientific evidence suggests otherwise. In the face of genetic determinism, Francis Collins of the HGP has responded by saying:

> I am somewhat repelled by the notion that we will reduce human beings to a parts list and a set of chemical reactions, that we will reduce ourselves to predetermined, DNA-driven robots, that love will become a series of chemical reactions and that God will become irrelevant. I'm interested in this project for the reason that healers have always been interested in learning more. So that they will be able to make sick people better. To argue that you shouldn't do this seems to be the most unethical.

We should have learned a long time ago that genetic determinism is a fraud. It is like neural determinism or any other form of biological determinism. Just as genetic uniqueness is not essential for human uniqueness, so a knowledge and understanding of the genetic basis of personality or disease does not lead to genetic determinism. In both cases, the environment plays a crucial role in making us what we are as people. The ways in which we respond to our circumstances and adapt to lives limited by genetic diseases or predispositions are central to the sort of people we are. We are not our genes, but we are people with certain genetic characteristics.

The Human Genome Diversity Project

The HGP is proving to be one of modern science's success stories, and yet it represents a composite genomic sequence of a mere handful of individuals. This fact was realized early on and a sister gene-mapping project, entitled the Human Genome Diversity Project (HGDP), was proposed in 1991 to overcome this shortcoming. The primary goal of the HGDP was to characterize and understand the genetic diversity of the world's peoples. This information would be of great anthropological value as well as providing insight into both normal variation and that responsible for inherited diseases. This is a truly ambitious undertaking, especially when one considers that the initial proposal aimed to collect and analyse DNA from somewhere between ten and one hundred thousand individuals representing five hundred of the world's five thousand or so different ethnic groups. The DNA was to be collected in concert with genealogical information and made available for worldwide scientific investigation.

All human genomes are remarkably similar, yet there are still important differences between any two individuals, differences which among other things are responsible either for susceptibility or resistance to various diseases. It is well known that different ethnic groups suffer from different diseases in different ratios. For example, there is an extremely high incidence of Tay Sachs disease in Jews of Eastern European origin, and of adult onset diabetes in the Old Order Amish. There is also preliminary evidence to suggest that some genes may confer protection against disease. Such 'useful' genes include those from a population in northern Italy who appear to be protected from some forms of heart disease, and prostitutes in Nairobi who seem to be immune to the HIV virus. It is hoped that differences in susceptibility between populations can be used to find genes, or genetically determined biochemical pathways, which can then be used as targets for therapy.

Despite the potential benefits on offer, opposition to the HGDP is rife. This stems mainly from indigenous peoples, who are concerned that they will be alienated from the control and use of their own genetic material and information. Indigenous groups believe that the HGDP views them as a means to an end, and is aimed primarily at benefiting scientific knowledge and big business, rather than assisting the indigenous peoples themselves. The fear is that the genetic reductionism inherent in this project threatens to destroy any mythologies of human origins different from those of the dominant world cultures.

Furthermore, many indigenous peoples consider that parts of their bodies such as hair, blood and DNA are sacred, and part of a group or tribal property which is not to be bought or sold without group consent. These issues are of particular concern for populations who have suffered discrimination and oppression in the past, and are now reluctant to do anything that could potentially increase this discrimination in the future.

Some scientists are equally critical of the HGDP on the grounds that it is poorly conceived. According to some vocal opponents, there is no such thing as genetically pristine populations in the world nowadays, and thus the HGDP will not be as lucrative for human evolution studies as first proposed. Further criticisms revolve around issues of confidentiality, and the belief that the HGDP will encourage racism.

Not surprisingly, the HGDP has obtained little funding due to the controversy surrounding its procedures and implications. The shaky financial position of the HGDP, coupled with poor political support has seen a reduction in the size and the scope of the project. Some feel that the HGDP can only proceed if those who further its objectives simultaneously respect the cultural beliefs of indigenous peoples. They should also publicly support the efforts of indigenous peoples to achieve respect and equality, and should ensure that both immediate and long-term economic benefits from research flow back to the groups taking part. If these warnings are not heeded, there are considerable doubts over the long-term viability of the project. In the midst of all the conflict, a number of biotechnology companies are conducting their own miniature versions of the HGDP in the search for useful genes that could lead to commercial products. By virtue of private funding these profit-driven companies have quietly sidestepped the ethical controversy plaguing the HGDP, and these same companies are likely to reap the medical benefits originally envisaged for the HGDP.

Genes, embryos and reproductive ethics

The areas covered in this chapter bring to a head the competing demands of medical treatment, efforts to protect the human embryo and more general human and humane interests. If we wish to resort to a picture of warfare, this is where we may well do so. It is also here that we encounter the possibly divergent demands of a pragmatic approach on the one hand, and of a more ideological approach on the other. And this is where a writer like me, who is both a scientist and a Christian, encounters mixed messages. This is not because I see inherent conflict between the two sides of what I am, nor that I wish to put out ambiguous messages. It is because others perceive that one cannot be both an advocate of reproductive science, and an upholder of embryonic interests. Christians rarely express concerns about indigenous peoples, and so a project like the HGDP tends to be ignored by Christian writers.

A major criticism of scientists like me is that we are seen to be upholding an autonomous medical empire, and then doing our best to speak with a Christian voice. To some, this reeks of compromise. Why not advocate an end to all manipulatory ventures on human embryos? Why not close the door on embryonic and genetic research, thereby protecting for ever the welfare of human embryos? The answer is simply that to do so would be to call a halt to any effort that might improve the welfare of human embryos. Surely, one cannot laud a situation whereby two-thirds of all embryos (and fetuses) never develop beyond the earliest stages of gestation? It is a strange world in which the death of human embryos on this scale is seen as preferable to limited research attempting to improve the welfare of future embryos or even adult humans.

Nevertheless, I share some of the concerns of critics of reproductive and genetic science. These have been provocatively expressed by C. Ben Mitchell, Senior Fellow at The Center for Bioethics and Human Dignity in the United States. In response to the HGP announcement in June 2000, he wrote, 'The bad news is that the science is being done in the context of what amounts to a moral dark age. Despite the status of 21st century science, our moral sensitivities are at a very low ebb ... we are dominated by technological giants and ethical pygmies ... Unless public scrutiny is radically enhanced and unless ethical vigilance is rigorously applied, this moment will be remembered in history as a very inglorious day of infamy.'[2]

The bleak language employed here prompts us to ask what ethical perspective would be required to transform the context within which this exciting work is being conducted. This quotation gives the impression that a Christian perspective is an entirely negative one about the HGP, let alone cloning. Is this a fair assessment, or does it reflect a theological perspective dominated by a particular viewpoint of the human embryo? Has a broader Christian framework been lost? To answer these questions, we need to stand back a little, and retrace our steps to other (and earlier) forms of technology.

The ethical and spiritual context within which technological developments of all hues have emerged – agriculture, the selective breeding of plants and animals, the nuclear industry, telecommunications, cyberspace – has probably not been significantly different from the one in which the genetic and reproductive technologies are appearing. Human history has been characterized by humans altering nature. True, until very recently this has been largely external to human life itself, although medical developments over hundreds of years have influenced the quality of human existence.

The new factor is the advent of the ability to modify human nature at the genetic and cellular levels; with this, science is able to intrude into the inner sanctuary of human life. Some feel that this is an intrusion into a sacred mystery of genetic givenness, a givenness that should be received with gratitude and never manipulated; hence the negative reaction to cloning in its various forms, and even to some extent to the HGP. But is DNA the stuff of sanctity? Is it any more sacrilegious to cut DNA than to cut living tissue as in conventional surgery? There is a deep feeling

---

[2] C. B. Mitchell, 'Genetic Renaissance in a Moral Dark Age'.

on the part of many, including theologians, that it is. Consequently, the genetic arena should be out of bounds to human
activity. Only God is allowed to move in this realm.

If this is the case, what does it tell us about God and about
DNA? Why should genes be any different from the proteins they
produce, or the tissues and organs to which the proteins contribute? All are 'matter', and all are essential constituents of living
organisms. God is concerned with every facet of living organisms, including, of course, human organisms. Under no circumstances are we to limit him to the genetic realm at the same time
as we exclude humans from that same realm. If God is sovereign
over all, he is sovereign over the genetic realm as he is over
human life, human community, and the ecosphere. Divine grace
and creativity are to be evident in all these realms, and human
creativity is to follow suit. If we can say that God works through
creation, there is no reason to say that he does not also work
through the basic processes described by biology and, therefore,
through genetic mechanisms.

For theologian Ronald Cole-Turner, treating DNA as matter
is not in itself sacrilegious, it is not beyond the legitimate reach of
science and, therefore, of manipulation. There is no reason why
God should not work through genetic technologies, and it is not
a mark of faithfulness to erect a wall of separation between them
and God. Consequently, Cole-Turner is comfortable with progress on deciphering the human genome.

If this is right, the next step is to affirm that genetic manipulation has the potential for extending the work of God, who routinely seeks genetic change as a means of his creative activity.
Moreover, he works through humans to achieve intentional
genetic change. One can even go further and state that God now
has more ways to create and to bring about fulfilment and
harmony, for example, through the medical and pharmaceutical
advances that will undoubtedly flow from the HGP over coming
years.

This is not carte blanche for humans to do anything in the
genetic realm, since whatever is done there has to be consistent
with the nature and purposes of God, who renews the whole

creation in anticipation of a new creation. To work this out in specific practical terms will require an enormous amount of ongoing theological and ethical discussion. What is beginning to emerge, though, is that the Christian's major task is not that of objecting to scientific developments, but of seeing them as one way in which God is demonstrating his grace through his creation.

A helpful Christian approach to genetic issues (as well as others in the biological realm) is that based on a stewardship ethic (see Reichenbach and Anderson, *On Behalf of God*). This is derived from the account in Genesis 2:15, where God appoints his stewards to work in, and take care of, God's garden. This works itself out in three ways (Gen. 1:28): to fill, rule, and care for the land. As stewards, humans are accountable to God for the manner in which they carry out these crucial tasks, and this necessitates an appreciation of the dimensions and limitations of their responsibility. What it does not do is automatically circumscribe the task and place huge areas off-limits. It is interesting that in exploring where the 'filling' command may lead, Reichenbach and Anderson interpret it in a qualitative manner, in that it could include helping humans become more disease-resistant, genetically superior, better adjusted to and able to cope with their environment. In other words, humans may well be encouraged to change the creation for the better should that prove possible.

This ethic recognizes technology as a gift to be used to benefit some, while not degrading or devaluing others. They write, 'To recognize that someone is in need biologically and to develop ways to meet those needs is not to demean their personhood; it is to recognize that they are persons for whom God has given us stewardship responsibility.'[3] They continue: 'We are to act on behalf of God, not out of human hubris. At the same time, as with all technology, justice requires that we make that which meets basic human needs available to persons regardless of their

---

[3] R. Reichenbach and V. E. Anderson, *On Behalf of God*, 187.

social position, consonant with the restrictions imposed by our limited resources.'[4]

What we have here is a mix of openness to future possibilities (based squarely on a theological base) and an awareness of our responsibilities for the welfare of human beings. Such an approach should lead to extreme care and caution about where science might take us, a scepticism about the limitations of our abilities and of our readiness to misuse them, and a restrained optimism about where genetic research will take us. Whether acknowledged or not, human beings are to act in a stewardship role, and it is the task of Christians to remind societies of this.

One of our great problems is our obsession with the normal, and this is something that could be accentuated by the HGP. On the other hand, as far more becomes known about individual genes and their consequences, we may come to learn that there is no genetic ideal to be approximated. Genetically, we are all flawed in various ways, and the interaction between combinations of genes that seem to be beneficial and those that seem to be flawed may be an intimate one. Even if there were a human ideal, it would be unattainable, since reproduction brings constant genetic variation (beware reproductive cloning!). To look for a genetically perfect human ideal is not only to treat humans as unchanging, but to ignore our human creatureliness and the randomness of all new genetic combinations.

Although these considerations appear to have taken us away from embryos, they constitute an invaluable starting point for all ventures into the genetic realm. They are also relevant for the HGDP, since our approach to the viewpoints of indigenous peoples is encompassed by these thoughts. The dignity and autonomy of indigenous groups are to be stressed by taking seriously their cultural identity, their views of their ancestors and history, the consequences of past discrimination, and their perspectives on how genetic material is to be handled and by whom.

---

[4] Ibid.

Questions for group discussion

1. Can you see any difference between human therapeutic cloning and human reproductive cloning?
2. Imagine a medical procedure which has considerable benefits and no substantial ethical problems, but the development of which has involved ethically debatable experiments. Would you be willing to make use of such a procedure?
3. Discuss what you consider to be the main ethical issues raised by stem cell research.
4. Do you feel that Christian perspectives throw any helpful light on human therapeutic cloning and stem cell technology? If so, what are they?
5. Can you envisage what it might be like to live in a post-HGP world, where medicine will have a very different character from what we are familiar with. Do you think this might have any influence on how we see God acting in our lives?
6. Work out what it might mean to say that God 'is sovereign over the genetic realm'.

Five

Biomedical Manipulation

The world of biomedical manipulation is upon us. No longer is it a scene from science fiction or a timid glimpse into a possible future – it is here, and we are both the manipulators and the manipulated. For Christians, this is the world in which Christ is to reign supreme; but how often do we think in these terms? What we have here is an uneasy tension between technologies that appear to be under human control, and God's world that is often seen as separate from the world of modern technology. While this has always been a false dichotomy, it is a far more pernicious one when humans are manipulated daily.

Fundamental to a Christian perspective on human life, including manipulated human life, is the notion that it is a gift from God, to be used wisely in his service and in the service of others. But how can this be true when even human beings themselves are being manipulated, whether at embryonic or fetal stages, or in adult life at the level of their emotions, behaviour or joints? To what extent is a gift from God open to being altered by God's own creations? Is this a new phenomenon, or are we simply confronting it at a more direct level today? In what ways can God be served by our using techniques that manipulate and change human beings like ourselves?

From one world to another

Let us imagine three communities.

Community one

Consider a community in which there is no sophisticated medicine of any description, and not much knowledge of public
health measures. Most people die by the age of forty, and two
out of three infants die before they are one year old. The community survives at a fairly basic level, and is very much in
touch with nature, the elements and religious forces. Much of
the ill health is ascribed to the actions of local gods, and any
good health and survival are put down to propitious forces
around them.

Community two

This is the same community some thirty years later. Western
influences are now being felt, various medical and surgical
procedures are available to the people, and public health measures are being instigated. Life expectancy has now risen to
around sixty years, and one out of three infants dies before the
age of one. The people are grateful for these changes, and
those who are Christian (owing to the presence of Christian
missionaries) are grateful to God for what has happened. Life
is no longer mere subsistence; it can be enjoyed and the skills
of the people can begin to flourish. The community has been
transformed beyond recognition.

Community three

It is another fifty years further into the future, and the same
community is now a far larger one. It has numerous contacts
with other similar communities and with the world at large.
High technology medicine is now widely available and prac-
tised within it. Most people expect to live to about seventy-
five years, and only one in fifty infants dies in the first year of
life. The people are healthy, although they are afflicted by
typical western disease patterns. They now look to medicine

for health and vigour, and relatively few of them see any relevance of God, or indeed of any religious ideals at all. They have become dependent upon medical (and many other forms of) technology, so much so that their horizons have become restricted by the prowess and limitations of biomedical technology. In material ways the community has a great deal, but in spiritual matters it gives the impression of being impoverished. It is somewhat lost, and ill at ease.

Would it have been better if these developments had not occurred, or if only some of them had taken place? Perhaps it would have been possible to freeze the community in a time warp between communities two and three. Perhaps ... but I doubt it. I have no hesitation in stating that the situation depicted in the second community is preferable to that depicted in the first. However, scientific and medical advances are capable of destroying as well as benefiting human aspirations, and this is where the problems highlighted by the third community come into view. As we look at this most recent community, we begin to get the feeling that medical technology may reach a stage where it causes more problems than it solves.

As we contemplate this third community, we have to ask whether technology inevitably leads to the loss of human and spiritual values. We begin to sense that a technological world may imperil the dignity and worth of human beings, and that the more widespread and efficient technology becomes, the more basic human values are seriously threatened. Is technology out of control, because self-centred human beings are incapable of directing it to other than their own selfish ends? Is technology already militating against any Christian agenda?

Christians with differing perspectives answer these questions in different ways. For some, there is no hope in a technological world, since such a world is implacably opposed to any Christian worldview. Christians who hold this position of *theological despair* are appalled at the direction already taken and likely to be taken even further in the biological and medical areas. Their concern is that developments in these spheres will lead to the manipulation of humans in ways that will inevitably detract from their Godlikeness.

An alternative response is that of *theological caution*, which accepts that technology can be harnessed for good as much as anything else in society can be harnessed for good. This stance does not pretend that technology will lead to an idealistic, brave new world, since it is accepted that technology can also be harnessed for evil. The good and evil applications are always intertwined, so that it is the responsibility of Christians to drive the applications that will enhance the human condition.

And then there is a third position, that of *theological optimism*, according to which technological achievements play an integral role in achieving some form of new world order. For instance, genetic technological advances will enable us to create more intelligent, attractive, and wiser human beings. On the whole, few Christians find this a compelling option.

The direction we take will have immense repercussions for our ability to handle the world of biological manipulation: total rejection, overeager acceptance, or a cautious weighing-up of the possibilities. As I examine my own response, I find that the position of theological caution is very much my position as a scientist and Christian, with the optimism of the scientific endeavour tempered by the Christian's far more pessimistic assessment of human nature. It is the scientist in me that leads me to question the stance of some theologians with their inherent conservatism. But by the same token it is the theologian in me that leaves me very uneasy by the bland allurements of rampant technological imperialism.

Theological caution refuses to lose sight of the crucial importance of human value. Under no circumstances are the dignity and worth of human beings to be sacrificed to technological imperialism; rather, all technology is to be directed towards upholding the value of humans as people created by God for his purposes. The direction taken by technology is totally dependent on either the responsibility or irresponsibility of people. Christians are to ensure, as far as they are able, that it is used to help people to improve their health and living standards and so make them better able to develop their potential as people created in the image and likeness of God.

As a Christian I am immensely grateful for so many of the scientific advances in the medical arena; this is technology at its best. Nevertheless, neither basic biomedical science nor its many technological applications in medicine exist in a spiritual and moral vacuum. Nor do they only exist in situations where the advances are going to be welcomed by everybody. There will be dissension, and there will be enormous ethical and moral challenges. But let us be clear about one thing: these challenges arise from the success of science and from the consequent degree of control this bestows upon humans. So many of the challenges arise from legitimate aspirations to help humanity rather than from untamed bravado and hubris.

This has been superbly illustrated by the scientific developments leading up to the cloning of Dolly, as recounted in Chapter 3. As we saw, the scientists' aims were to understand the process of differentiation in cells, and also to explore how cloning allied with genetic modification can open up new technological vistas in the pharmaceutical and agricultural areas. This is serious science and responsible technology, and however great the challenges of this and allied work may be, we would be exceedingly foolish to reject it out of hand for spurious ethical or theological reasons.

On to a future world

Interesting as these communities are, they take us only as far as the end of the twentieth century. We now need to look beyond this time to well into the twenty-first century, with a fourth community.

Community four

In this community technology has become indispensable for all human activities. Forty percent of babies are born as a result of some form of artificial fertilization, the use of artificial organs is commonplace (although pig organs are still quite commonly used for transplantation purposes), the use of animal and human cloning for therapeutic purposes is routine, and a small number of cloned individuals are found in most towns (although you would have no idea who they are). Tissue transplantation to alleviate the worst effects of Alzheimer's disease is regarded as normal, and some familial forms of the disease are prevented by genetic manipulation. Parkinson's disease can be cured in its early stages by neurotransmitter chips implanted in patients' brains. Genetic enhancement is successful in eliminating some personality traits, so that rage and anger can be 'removed' during gestation. This community is also a cyberspace community, where virtual worlds have transformed the nature of time and place; everyone is instantly accessible, and yet face-to-face human relationships have largely disappeared. It is becoming a lonely community.

This manipulated community sounds strange, and yet meeting the people and talking with them shows how normal they are. Their interests, worries and hopes are very much like those of the third community, even if they expect technological 'fixes' to almost everything. And yet, even they realize that these fixes do not solve all their problems. The future is as uncertain as ever it was, and the technology can let them down; it goes wrong from time to time, and on occasion the results are unexpected. Sometimes there are even tragedies. And in the end, everyone in the fourth community withers and dies, although some rebel against death far more than they would have done fifty years before. Death is far more of an ugly intrusion than it used to be.

For this community of the future, biomedical technology has ceased to be optional, even if it ever was. As these people contemplate their society they have come to realize that there is no point in discussing whether some piece of technology should or should not be developed: it will be developed. The question is how it should be used, and that is ultimately the essence of all debates.

Community four, of course, is the world we inhabit, or will shortly inhabit. Those features absent today will be with us in ten, twenty, or thirty years' time. We now need to consider where Christian reflection might take us in coming to grips with this strange new world.

Is technology threatening God's image in humans?

One of the fundamental tenets of Christian theology is that humans are created in the image and likeness of God. It is this that is seen as distinguishing human beings from all other creatures and plants. There is something special about us, and this is one way of expressing it. Living in a pre-technological era, John Calvin wrote that 'God looks upon himself ... and beholds himself in men [people] as in a mirror.' This suggests that as God looks on people, he recognizes that they are icons (images) of himself: in humans God finds his own perfections and characteristics mirrored back to himself. From this it follows that when we see a human being we see a creature who delights God by mirroring him. In this sense we mirror each other, since we are like each other, regardless of our abilities or disabilities, our distinction or lack of it, our good health or debilitating ill health.

The phrase 'image of God' occurs principally in the early chapters of Genesis (1:26, 27; 9:6), as well as in a small number of New Testament passages (1 Cor. 11:7; 2 Cor. 4:4; Col. 1:15). There is also reference to people being in the likeness of God (Jas. 3:9). Other New Testament passages refer to the transformation of Christians into the image of Christ (Rom. 8:29; 2 Cor. 3:18; Col. 3:10).

The image of God has been interpreted in a variety of ways historically: to refer to the spirituality, rationality and morality of human beings; to their dominion over creation; to their capacity to enter into relationship with God; and to physical attributes such as their bodies and upright posture. These capacities taken together in Christian thinking bestow upon humans their uniqueness – it is not their genetic uniqueness, which is not very striking anyway. Nor does it lie in any uniqueness of their nerve cells, neurotransmitters or trophic factors, all of which are unnervingly similar from one species to another.

Alongside this concept we can place another, and this is that human life is a gift from God (Gen. 4:1; 16:2; 29:31, 32; 30:22, 23; Ruth 4:13). The beginning of human life, from fertilization onwards, is viewed as an act of creation in which both humans and God have their essential roles to play. It is not purely a human act, from which God can be totally excluded, nor is it a spiritual transaction devoid of human participation; it is the gift of new life to the one who has come into existence, a gift that springs from human decision-making and human actions, whether responsible or irresponsible, whether natural or artificial. In the Old Testament, God is frequently seen as opening or closing the wombs of individuals, not as illustrations of biological bravado, but within a context of faith. What is relevant here is not obstetrics, but God's purposes, his gift of new human life, and the rewards of faith.

These are far from new concepts, but they may take on new dimensions when human action is directed at modifying the bodies and brains, and therefore the self-image, of human beings themselves. As artificial devices move from the external environment to the internal environment, from the world around us to the world within us, are we being forced to see ourselves differently? Indeed, is there some profound sense in which our likeness to God is diminished, and even God's role in bringing us into being usurped when the artificial begins to take precedence over the natural?

Enormous care is required in addressing these issues, since in Christian terms human beings have been given dominion over the world (Gen. 1:26–8; Ps. 8:6–8). They are to be stewards of the whole environment (Gen. 2:15), utilizing their capabilities for the good of all – other creatures, the physical world, and the human community. Without this dominion and stewardship, humans would still be at the level of the first community. But that is no longer the case.

Humans have tinkered with nature for hundreds if not thousands of years. They have intruded into nature throughout recorded human history, whether it has been by draining swamps infested with malaria-bearing mosquitoes or by using antibiotics. Nature has given us genetic combinations that lead to Huntington's disease, diabetes, and heart disease, but few would argue that these particular combinations are to be welcomed and preserved. Medicine has traditionally done its best to cope with these conditions, and the concern normally expressed has not been the nature of the intrusion itself, but whether the intrusion enhances or diminishes the human condition.

Few object to the spectacular advances of medicine in controlling and combating the common diseases, since these advances are welcomed as improving human health and well-being. Furthermore, we continue to be appalled when children die of a variety of cancers, when men in their prime are struck down by heart attacks, when young women succumb to breast cancer or cervical cancer, or when old people are dreadfully transformed by Alzheimer's disease. But these conditions are only the tip of the iceberg, since there are infinitely more people in the Two-Thirds World who are tragically afflicted by diseases that have largely disappeared from the rest of the world: malaria, tuberculosis, trachoma, and common respiratory and gastrointestinal diseases. High-quality health care and stringent public health measures are essential, not optional extras.

Nature is neither to be worshipped as if it were some unchanging given, not is it to be elevated to some untouchable status as if it were fixed and immutable. Since humans have been given stewardship of the created order, the crucial issue is to determine the sort of interference with nature that will advance human welfare, at the same time respecting the dimensions of what it means to be human. This requires a great deal of enlightened ethical discernment, and an awareness of the tentative path along which we are travelling.

We have every reason to be cautious over the directions of technology, but our caution has to be balanced against the destructive forces of nature out of control. Christians would do well to examine the effects of both, and then to direct their efforts at seeing that the good of the interference outweighs the evil of both interference gone wrong and of nature unrestrained.

The crucial word here is 'control'. Cloning, genetic manipulation and especially genetic targeting, and the whole of the HGP, point towards an ever-increasing precision of control of what we are biologically as human beings. The ability to pinpoint genes, what they do and how they go wrong, the ability to reprogram a genome, the ability to switch on genes that under normal circumstances would have been switched off during differentiation, and the ability to utilize fibroblasts as the source of cloned animals and a whole array of tissues and even organs, are all examples of precise control and of a new dimension to biotechnology and molecular medicine. Such techniques will liberate biology from constraints that once seemed inviolable, and will transform medical practice and human expectations.

Theologically, this presents us with an immense challenge because we have to determine where we see God's hand at work. Is it in the uncertain and the mysterious, and/or in what human beings can control? As cloning and genetic engineering offer the prospect of removing much randomness and uncertainty, we have to determine whether God is the God of the controlled parts of human life as well as of the uncertain and uncontrolled parts of human existence (Chapter 4). Working from the premiss that God is sovereign over all and that his common grace applies to all, I would argue that his concerns are universal and that he sustains everything. Any 'God of the gaps' approach, which sees him in only that which cannot be explained leads to a pitiful diminishment of our conception of him. We should rejoice in increased control, realizing that this brings with it an awesome responsibility, which can only be fulfilled as it is undertaken in dependence upon God.

But we have to go further, and ask whether there are limits to the extent of the manipulation that could or should be undertaken on individuals. Is there a boundary between being images of God and not being images of God? This may sound like a macabre science fiction scenario of part-human, part-beast dimensions, in which the beast overwhelms the human. The reality will be far more subtle than this, depending possibly on radical genetic modification, multi-organ replacements, or the transplantation of brain cells from other species. The concern of some is that manipulation of this order will actually alter the moral status of those who have undergone manipulation. Instead of reflecting God they will reflect their human creators; instead of being able to live as moral agents they will be the hand-maidens of those who have manipulated them.

These are disturbing possibilities, and it is hardly surprising that they elicit repugnance in many people, including many Christians. The difficulty here is that we are moving in uncharted territory, and future scenarios of this kind are always troubling. Perhaps we can throw some light on to these possibilities by probing them and asking pertinent questions. Would these modi-fied individuals still be able to respond to their world, to other people and to God? Would they still be capable of understanding and of having meaningful relationships with others in the human community, of having values and hopes, of planning for the future, of demonstrating love and compassion, of making choices, of worshipping, and of enjoying pizzas? These capaci-ties and many others like them make up the repertoire of human behaviour, and point in some measure to what it means to be 'in the image and likeness of God'. Even now human beings vary enormously in their capacities and limitations, mostly due to natural variation, some to pathological conditions, and some to technological manipulation; but we do not doubt their human-ness and their oneness with others in the human community.

On the other hand, were any individuals to be so modified that they could no longer function in these ways, their status would indeed have been imperilled. Continuing in the science fiction realm, one can imagine individuals created without cere-bral hemispheres, serving simply as collections of living organs, but one has to ask what would be the point of using sophisticated technologies to provide such an inefficient source of organs. No moral society would tolerate such actions, and no rational society would see any virtue in proceeding like this. The ardent and ongoing debate over the use of organs from anencephalics, and the treatment of those in a persistent vegetative state, is testimony to this. Not only this; the moral status of individuals is already seriously challenged in far more mundane ways: for instance, by the excessive use of behaviour-modifying drugs, by solitary confinement for long periods of time, by vicious forms of torture, and by a host of unethical practices.

Any procedures or practices that take from individuals the capacity to make choices and act upon them, and that restrict their value systems or their awareness of themselves and others, do indeed imperil the essence of what it means to be human. This is because they impinge on the freedom to be human, something vital to the capacity of people to act as God's agents. Nevertheless, if this freedom is retained and if individuals retain the capacity to be themselves and to express themselves, no matter how technologically manipulated they may be, they will continue to reflect the crucial relational features of a personal God.

Manipulation in action

Reproductive cloning and embryos

We have already seen that the cloning of human individuals has emerged as one of the most detested of technological procedures at the beginning of human life. I presented a scenario in Chapter 1 where cloning was accepted within a society, leading to the existence of cloned human individuals within that society. In that chapter I considered how we should treat them. Would they be second-class citizens with an inferior status to all other humans? What I want to do in this section is answer these questions by reference to the embryo and the way in which it develops.

As far as I can see, once any new individuals have commenced to develop, whether or not fertilization has taken place, subsequent development as embryo and then fetus, will be the same. Consequently, an embryo brought into existence by cloning will be indistinguishable from any other human embryo. This is straightforward scientific fact. And so, if we argue that a naturally fertilized human embryo shows us something of the handiwork of God, so too will a cloned human embryo. The beginnings of God-given life will be evident in both types of human embryo. If it is argued that fertilized human embryos bear God's image, it follows that cloned human embryos will also bear God's image. Therefore, once implantation in a woman's uterus has taken place (or is expected to take place) cloned embryos should be treated exactly as one would treat naturally fertilized embryos. This places upon us a responsibility to take further the development of cloned as well as naturally fertilized embryos.

If one argues that a prior moral commitment should be made to treat human embryos as persons or potential persons, it seems to me that this applies regardless of whether or not fertilization has occurred. In my view, the treatment of fertilized and cloned embryos must be equivalent; once in existence, the two are parallel. This does not justify cloning as a technique, any more than it justifies every action resulting in natural fertilization or every use of the artificial reproductive technologies. Those are separate moral decisions.

While these arguments do not justify the cloning of individuals, they lead to an acceptance of the worth and value of any cloned embryos or individuals who may be brought into existence. Once a new individual is recognized as developing towards human individuality, the process that brought about that development is irrelevant. The moral status of fertilized and cloned embryos will be identical.

Hence, even in this extreme form of biomedical manipulation, what one ends up with is an individual of identical moral status to any naturally fertilized individual. A cloned individual is as much a creature made in the image and likeness of God as is any other individual, and is as deserving of God's care and protection as any other. Not only this; there is no reason to believe that God will not call cloned individuals to be his servants and to be leaders in his church.

Therapeutic cloning and embryos

But would we be treating cloned and fertilized embryos equally if the cloned embryos had been produced to serve as a source of tissues, that is, as part of a therapeutic cloning venture? We are not now dealing with individuals who are to be treated equally, but with the earliest stages in embryonic development. This forces us to return to an old chestnut: the status of the human embryo, the very early embryo (the blastocyst) in this case. We have seen in previous chapters, that biomedical manipulation is increasingly focusing on the first four to five days of human development, and it is this focus that causes so many people so much trouble. Scientists will not leave the human embryo alone. We have seen why this is so, and in purely scientific and clinical terms that may be easy to understand; but will it only be made possible by dramatically altering our whole outlook on human beings and even on what we think human existence is all about? Is this the Achilles heel of biomedical manipulation, and is this where it should stop?

Traditional definitions of the embryo use as their starting point the phenomenon of fertilization, since an embryo has usually been considered to come into existence once a sperm and egg have fused. This is not an instantaneous process, and it raises many fascinating scientific questions. Nevertheless, it had been recognized as the definitive starting point of a new individual until, that is, cloning came along. Cloning (SCNT) involves the reprogramming of one cell type to produce all the other cell types necessary for the development of a complete organism. Fertilization is bypassed, and a blastocyst with its inner cell mass is created; the aim of this form of cloning together with stem cell technology is to obtain specific tissues from some of these inner cell mass cells. There will be no new individual because the normal processes that would have given rise to a complete individual will have been altered to produce the desired tissues and nothing else. However, theoretically, a new individual could have been produced, although this would not be the intention and would not be allowed to occur.

This is an intense form of biomedical manipulation, which has changed the direction of normal cellular development quite dramatically – in bypassing fertilization, and in redirecting processes to produce one or a few tissue types rather than all the tissues of the body. This forces us to ask whether there is any ethical distinction between a blastocyst generated from egg and sperm and a cloned blastocyst, and also between a blastocyst on its way to forming a whole individual and one that will give rise to, say, muscle tissue. The second blastocyst in each of these pairs is the result of human manipulation which has as its goal some form of therapy or research. A decision has been taken to use human blastocysts in this way; there is no intention of bringing a new human life into existence, since the blastocysts will not be implanted in a woman's uterus.

This is control of a very high order. For some it is despicable control, since it is grossly abusing human persons. For others, the blastocyst brought into existence with the intention of giving rise to tissues rather than an individual is exquisite science that may open up immense new paths in medical treatment. This is human creativity at its pinnacle; but is it creativity being used to uphold and advance the welfare of others, or is it being put to ghastly immoral uses? I find this difficult to answer. Simply, I am unsure what the best answer is, since the circumstances surrounding these blastocysts are different from anything else we are used to. They appear to have far more in common with animal research tissues than with human embryos on their way to becoming like us, a consequence of decisions we will have taken. We will have made them like this. To me, this is the crux of the debate. Should we do this?

One approach is to say that, once we have artificially created and manipulated human blastocysts at our disposal in the laboratory, the normally accepted controlling moral values for dealing with blastocysts have disappeared, and a new set of values has to be elaborated. An alternative perspective is that we should never place ourselves in a position where we are faced with such a predicament, which should always be out of bounds to human beings. The artificial production of blastocysts for treatment and/or research purposes should never be contemplated.

Unfortunately, there are huge unknowns on both fronts. Can we be sure that artificially produced blastocysts are equivalent to human persons? Do we know the extent of the scientific vistas open to humankind? I suggest that in both cases the answers are 'no'. To treat human blastocysts as sacred and untouchable not only precludes any research on them, but sets them apart from all other human tissue and material. Equally, treating blastocysts as of less interest than any other human tissue, also sets them apart. Attempts either to elevate or demean their status unduly are flawed and doomed to failure. Scientifically, there may be other ways of achieving just as much without utilizing human blastocysts; this is a distinct possibility, although so much of what we currently know about early human development has come over the past hundred years or so from studies of human embryos. We are walking on very uncertain ground, scientifically, ethically and theologically, and all concerned should be prepared to admit this.

We are confronted with perplexity and with our own hubris. We dare not treat lightly even blastocysts, those most insignificant of human forms. If we do, the liberation from biological constraints that we so avidly long for may prove less of a social and moral liberation than we had hoped. But where does this leave us?

Christians do not have any insights on blastocysts that are unavailable to others; what they do have is an emphasis on the dignity and worthwhileness of all human life, including prenatal life. This recognizes that determined efforts are to be made to improve all human life, a thrust that is balanced by the restraint imposed by the inclusion of prenatal stages. What this balance means is that we cannot ignore the possibilities opened up by scientific developments for improving human welfare, but neither can we ride roughshod over even the earliest stages of human existence. There is no escaping the tension between these two emphases, a tension that reaches its height when confronted by the possibilities opened up by artificially created and manipulated blastocysts.

We can refuse to contemplate creating such blastocysts, for the very best of reasons – an eminently worthy position. Or if society decides to go in this direction it should be made abundantly clear that humans have taken upon themselves a momentous role that should be both carefully directed and highly circumscribed. Free reign should never be given to human beings to deal lightly with early human development, even artificially created and manipulated blastocysts.

Blurring species boundaries

The prospects of xenotransplantation, that is, transplanting organs from one species to another, probably from pigs to humans, have elicited considerable debate for some time. The problems are well known, although most of these revolve around the possibility of transferring dangerous viruses from the donor species to the host species. But there is also a broader question, and this is whether we know enough to cross species boundaries with impunity. Do genes have a particular significance in that they determine the essence of any one species, and does moving genes around destroy the integrity of species as natural kinds? These appear to be legitimate concerns, even though some argue that psychological and philosophical questions should be ignored in order to concentrate solely on the scientific debate. It is also salutary to realize that the vast majority of the genes found in the human genome are also found in the chimpanzee genome, with not many less in the mouse genome, and even in various plant genomes. But this still leaves queries and fears about blurring species boundaries. What about this?

Consider first the use of organs that serve primarily mechanical functions, like kidneys, hearts or lungs. In clinical terms, the transplantation of a kidney can be compared ethically to the use of dialysis equipment, since the therapeutic goals are comparable, regardless of whether the kidney comes from a human or pig. It is this common goal that should determine the ethical issues, rather than the relative degree of chimaerism involved. For instance, if an organ is taken from a pig genetically altered to suppress rejection, only a few out of many thousand human genes would be inserted into the pig. Any blurring of species boundaries would be minimal.

On the other hand, the transplantation of nerve cells from one species to another may potentially affect personality and person-hood, and could possibly have implications for the nature of patients' humanity. Is this type of procedure substantially differ-ent from other standard treatments such as neurosurgery or psychosurgery, which are generally regarded as ethical when carried out with a therapeutic rationale?

It is difficult to see how the ethical issues associated with xenotransplantation would be different from any allotransplan-tation (between individuals of the same species) undertaken in the neural area. A nerve cell's significance stems from its func-tional capabilities and from the connections and circuits of which it is a part. Consequently, it is probably more important neurobiologically to concentrate on the brain region being studied, and on the character and extent of the nerve cells, growth factors and transmitters being transplanted, than on whether the neural cells are of human, porcine or rodent origin. There may well be no significant difference between nerve cells from different species, since it is the environment and context within which they develop and function that determine an indi-vidual's ultimate personality. Experience with neural allo-transplants to date (to alleviate conditions such as Parkinson's and Huntington's diseases) do not suggest that the presence of another human's neural cells inside our brain makes us different people, at least not in the sense that worries people philosophi-cally. The central question should be whether the individual patient will be enhanced or diminished as a person by xenotransplantation.

This is the fundamental issue from which we cannot escape, and we always return to it. There is no way in which human beings will cease being human by introducing into them a small number of genes from another species. Whether or not this is a good thing to do has strong scientific and ethical overtones. But I do not believe it has any specific repercussions for Christian thinking. This form of biomedical manipulation has to be assessed in scientific, ethical and social terms, rather than in theological ones.

Enhancing human characteristics

The possibility of enhancing an individual's abilities, as opposed to rectifying something that has gone wrong, uncovers important considerations. Is the notion of enhancement antipathetic to Christian goals? In order to work through this question, let me take as an example enhancement genetic engineering, which would involve the insertion of a gene into an individual in an attempt to improve on a particular trait in that individual. The aim in this case would be modification (improvement) of a *healthy* individual in a permanent manner. This is similar to providing growth hormone to normal individuals in order to improve their sporting prowess. What is happening here is that genetic engineering would be employed, not in the treatment of a disease, but in an attempt to improve a perfectly healthy individual. Christian concerns emerge forcibly here, since any attempt to improve upon what is given may simply demonstrate rebellion against a bodily pattern ordained by God. In acting in this way, we may be setting ourselves up as creators of a new pattern rather than as stewards of God's creation. Alternatively, quite a different perspective contends that, if we are able to enhance human characteristics, we should do so as God's agents (see Chapter 3). The basic thought in this instance is that the present human form is not perfect, but is eminently capable of what could be viewed as God-ordained improvement.

Underlying these different perspectives is a fundamental query: what theological evidence do we have that the structure and functioning of the human body reflect a divinely determined pattern? Here we have another basic theological consideration. How do we read the creation account in Genesis? Does it point to a completed creation or a transformative process? I have dealt with this in previous chapters, where we saw that our answers have implications for how we judge techniques such as genetic modification in humans and human cloning. What is required is consistency between our theology and our practice of science and medicine.

I have previously indicated that I have difficulty in completely separating the two viewpoints into competing perspectives. For me, both are able to make helpful contributions. It would be foolhardy to think that we could come up with a totally new pattern of human anatomy and physiology. By the same token, to accept human functioning as we know it, with its sometimes deleterious viruses, rampaging bacteria, and destructive cancerous growths, is to give in to evil and suffering. The way forward must lie somewhere between these two extremes.

Similarly, notions of enhancement may not be clear-cut. It is easy to dismiss enhancement when it is little more than striving after ephemeral beauty, questionable intelligence and dubious business acumen. But enhancement may amount to far more than this. Imagine we can improve an individual in the sense that they will not suffer from heart disease in fifty years' time. When the genetic enhancement is carried out, the individual – albeit possibly an embryo – is healthy, and in the absence of the enhancement would continue to be healthy for many years. Is the avoidance of heart disease at the age of fifty years an improvement? The answer has to be 'yes', since disease is being replaced by health. Should such enhancement be condemned? I doubt it. What, then, if one could improve an individual's athletic performance by gene replacement? This is improvement in the sense that good exercise and coaching constitute enhancement. Ill health does not come into this; but by the same token is there anything wrong with exercise and coaching? Not in principle, although there may be when the exercise and coaching become excessive.

What emerges is that even genetic enhancement is not such a clear-cut issue as sometimes envisaged. Although there may be substantial reasons to be wary of it, it cannot be lightly dismissed. What are the reasons for attempting it? Do the anticipated changes amount to improvement in any meaningful sense, or are they ephemeral? Are they directed at benefiting the individual or at serving someone else's interests? What requires careful assessment are the motives and goals of those who advocate any form of enhancement, and of the societies in which this occurs. The hormonal enhancement of East German athletes twenty years ago was abhorrent at the time, and is now reaping a bitter legacy in chronic ill health. That example illustrates all that can be wrong with enhancement when it ignores basic ethical parameters, and thereby abuses the people being enhanced for the benefit of others. All enhancement, now and in the future, need not be of this order, and considerable theological reflection will be required to place it in a God-centred context.

Genetic manipulation

The previous discussion of therapeutic cloning was nothing more than a foretaste of future issues, since, dramatic as it may seem to us now, it does not involve gene modification. This would be far more intrusive than therapeutic cloning and stem cell technology, since it would involve the modification of embryos to be implanted in a woman's uterus for further development into a future individual. After all, the characteristics and welfare of future individuals will be at stake when their genes have been manipulated in some way (even when this has been for the highest of motives). The drive here will be therapy, the alleviation of illness or the prevention of genetically based conditions. The whole realm of genetic manipulation is closely tied in with the HGP, and it is this, with its roots in therapy, that makes genetic manipulation almost inevitable.

Nonetheless, the genetic realm is a potentially dangerous one, and this is a salutary reminder to all who would indulge in its possible excesses. Genetic knowledge confronts us in a poignant way with ambiguity. On the one hand, we want to know all: our curiosity drives us to search and to keep on searching. Genetics shows us much about why we are as we are, but it also enables us to know something about what we will be like in the future. And it is this ability to look into the future and control what may happen in the future that is so alluring. But is it too alluring, and will too much self-knowledge lead to a loss of control over our own lives?

Alongside this ambiguity goes another, and that is the prospect of greatly increased control over people's lives and all-pervasive intervention in their lives. Such control and intervention may be used exclusively for good, but there is always the prospect that this may not be the case, and we recoil from that prospect. Here, then, is ambiguity once more: we may be able to control others, but they too will be able to control us and may not do it with the best of intentions.

The control envisaged for technology raises the spectre of technology out of control and abused. Although human beings are capable of understanding, control and enormous responsibility, we are prone to debasing our understanding, to exercising control selfishly, and to acting irresponsibly. The ease with which we misuse our many abilities lies at the heart of our problems, giving rise as it does to strife, enmity, selfish excesses, inequality and injustice.

It is appropriate, therefore, that we are concerned lest biomedical manipulation is abused, since we find ourselves in a broken world where the images of God are in rebellion against God's authority. What then can Christians do who are as much part of a technologically dominated world as anyone else? Of one thing we can be certain, we cannot escape into some non-technological corner where we will be left in peace. That is escapism, not biblical faithfulness. We are 'in' the world of biomedical technology, but we are not to be 'of' it. Such a general caution is interesting, but what might it mean in practice?

Searching for a Christian ethos

A Christian ethos is characterized by the motivation and aspirations of the people of faith, rather than by some outward conformity to regulations regarding which forms of technology are or are not acceptable. This is something we find intensely difficult to grapple with, because a pure heart is far more demanding than well-regulated conformity (Jas. 2:8–17). It is, therefore, to the virtues that we must turn. How are we going to live in a world even more dominated by technology?

The power to heal, which has undergirded medicine throughout its history, remains central to the aspirations with which I have been dealing. The accomplishments of biomedical technology stem from the power it bestows on humans to alter the course of nature. Without this power, it is nothing, and herein lies the problem: power can be used wisely, but power can also corrupt. From this there is no escape, since this dichotomy is built into the human condition with its dimensions of grandeur and glory, but also of finiteness and fallenness.

More specifically, when confronted by the sort of biomedical manipulation with which I have been dealing, further sets of caution are called for. We are to beware of an ethic of perfectionism, with its longing for ideal children and ideal adults. Most of us most of the time long for this, and yet it will always let us down, for neither children nor adults are ever perfect. While longing for the best and highest, we have to be realistic, in the sense that when our children, our neighbours, and our companions fail to live up to idealistic expectations, we are to provide them with nurture, care and hope.

Perfection has no place in an inherently imperfect world, and technology will not provide it. Such a goal is resolutely at odds with any Christian perspective, which seeks to welcome all into a community of hope, including the imperfect and the battered. And so we live with tension at this point. Unfortunately, many grand technological vistas allude to perfectibility, improving humans in some unspecified ways (although this was more to the fore in the mid-twentieth century than today). Not only is this at odds with the integration and wholeness of a Christian ethos, but there is also a further problem: would we really want perfection, with its message that challenges will disappear for ever? Do we really want total technological control, even were such control ever attainable? As we contemplate even the merest possibility that this could ever occur, we begin to get the feeling that it would be the complete antithesis of all that human existence means. Too much control would alter our self-identity, regardless of the nature of that control, since all wonder at the nature of what is 'given' would disappear. We could make all things, and there would be nothing outside the bounds of human imagination. Nothing would be 'by chance', nothing would lie in the future, since the future would be constructed by those in the present. Of course, such a world will never come, but neither should we hanker after such a world, which is at compete odds with everything within the Christian conception. It is this technological vision that we need to rebuff rather than the details of some of the issues I have been discussing.

Such general considerations remind us of our frailty. If it is true that, as soon as we are able to do something, it must be done, then we have limited the ethical possibilities open to us. This is because we have lost a fundamental element of what we are, and of what we ought to be. Does this mean we should say 'no' to possible future developments in biomedicine? I think we should be able to do so, although in practice it may be more of a decision for each of us as individuals, rather than something societies as a whole decide to do. To say 'no' only becomes possible when we accept that human value is not dependent upon such developments, but emanates from God who is truly our Creator and sustainer. This is a serious matter for Christians; it is also a challenge for them to show others what it means to be human, as people in the image and likeness of God.

A great deal of caution and humility is required, because any tampering with fundamental biological processes is tinged with scientific, let alone theological, problems. There is much we do not know, and there is much over which we have only limited control. It is as important to know when to stop as when to continue. We need to recognize the extent of our ignorance and of our foolhardiness, as much as of our knowledge and our wisdom, and this applies both at the scientific and moral levels. A bravado approach emphasizes our knowledge but not our ignorance, whereas a fearful approach emphasizes only our ignorance. What is needed is a balance between human grandeur, and human limitation. What is needed is a critical assessment of the state of the science, careful moral reasoning regarding the values at stake, and a theological input that identifies and upholds the dignity of all participants. This, I believe, is the duty of those who have an inside knowledge of the science of modern biology and modern medical practice. For Christians, to refuse to face up to biology and its implications by criticizing every new development is to renounce their duty as the Lord's people. This is a tragedy because it cuts off any contribution they can make to this aspect of the modern world, and to the values that should inform biomedical debate. Christians do not have all the answers, and they have an enormous amount to learn. But they also have a theological and philosophical base that is urgently needed in postmodern, secular societies.

In all their dealings, Christians are to act humbly, realizing their dependence upon God. They are to recognize that they are not their own, but that they belong to God to be used according to his purposes. They have to sift through the mire of doomsday predictions on the one hand, and narcissistic expectations on the other, and emerge with a position that is faithful to biblical teaching and that glorifies God. They may not agree with the direction societies have taken, yet they have to continue to be part of those societies, to be a light for them and to serve a prophetic role.

As we look forward to the world of the first twenty to thirty years of the twenty-first century, there will be ever-increasing human control and biological interventions. Some of us will shy away from some of these. And yet, we need to remember that human lives have been manipulated and transformed in very crude ways for very many years, and sophisticated technological procedures may represent nothing worse; indeed, they will probably represent something infinitely better. The responsibility of Christians is to ensure as far as they are able that technological procedures are directed towards good ends, ones that will enhance human lives and give a clearer indication of what God meant life to be like. This is the scientific, the medical and the spiritual challenge that faces everyone.

Questions for group discussion

1. Discuss the pros and cons of living in each of the four communities. Which would you choose to live in? On what grounds do you make your decision?
2. To what extent do you think that we and our societies are in a position to reject the development of any new technologies? Do you think Christians should have a role to play in this type of decision making?
3. What differences, if any, are there between improving health through public health measures and improving health through genetic means?
4. Is an increase of human control in the genetic realm a threat to God's sovereignty? Or should it be welcomed as a means by which God's purposes can be enhanced?
5. Talk about the differences between therapy and enhancement. Should Christians be opposed to all forms of enhancement? If so, why?

Six

Brave New People

In the previous chapters I have covered the major issues surrounding cloning in general, and human reproductive and therapeutic cloning in particular. My hope is that I have been successful in showing why there is such turmoil surrounding these procedures and also how we might begin to approach them. I have not intended to suggest that there are ready-made answers – there are not, regardless of our starting point. I have also aimed to place cloning within the much larger context provided by other related biomedical procedures at the beginning of life, especially stem cell technology and the HGP. What has emerged is that these all play a part in what I have referred to as biomedical manipulation, the control of some of the fundamental processes that make us the sort of beings we are as individual people. In this final chapter I shall talk around these issues, retracing some old ground, but also aiming to provide a helpful framework for tackling these and related processes. If there is one thing of which we can be certain, it is that the type of developments we have encountered in this book are not a one-off. The world of 2020 and the world of 2060 will still be debating and struggling with revolutions in biology, revolutions writers in those future times will have just as much trouble with as we have today. Christians, too, will continue to be perplexed and troubled by them, since those developments (whatever they may be) will prove as taxing as anything confronting us in the early years of the first decade of the twenty-first century.

A salutary story

A scientist had reached the top of his profession. He had a prestigious professorship at a well-known university; he had numerous large research grants; he was repeatedly invited to speak at international conferences; and his papers were widely quoted. There was even talk that he was a serious contender for a Nobel Prize. But this scientist lacked something. Although his local hospital kept banks of cloned tissues for him, in case he needed these tissues following illness, he knew that one day he would die and people would quickly forget all about him. And so he decided to have himself cloned, so that the next generation would have some idea of what he had been like.

This was arranged: a paid 'surrogate' would provide the egg, and carry the fetus to term. She would also look after the child for the first seven years of his life. The scientist would visit the child whenever he had time.

But the scientist was devastated. His 'child' was quite unlike what he had expected, being mainly interested in playing sport and computer games, and with little apparent aptitude for science. Even worse, he wanted to have nothing to do with the scientist, who was neither his father nor brother.

The disillusioned scientist could have started all over again, and had another clone of himself produced. But he began to realize that he had become so focused on himself and his own achievements that he had lost sight of his true contribution to humanity.

What we have here is the longing for immortality, first in the form of protecting oneself from illness in the future, and second from a fate that befalls most of us: being lost to memory, simply disappearing from the face of this earth. Neither type of longing depends on cloning; we all try to accomplish these things in different ways, and people have attempted to do them through-out human history. But cloning seems to have an efficiency unknown to all previous generations.

The manufacture of tissues that may come in useful in some future illness has been a power unknown to us up to now, when we have had nothing to fall back on or, at best, have had to contend with possible rejection of organs and tissues taken from other people. There seems to be no virtue in relying on such inef-ficient methods when others become available – as long, that is, as no important ethical boundaries are breached. But it is equally important that we do not place too much store by these approaches. For many of us they will never be of any relevance, because we shall not need them medically. Of far greater signifi-cance, though, is the realization that most people in the world will not be able to benefit from them no matter how efficient they become. This is for the sad and simple reason that people in most countries of the world will lack the financial or medical resources to make use of them. Cloning and any medical benefits it may bring will be beyond their reach, just as most other high technol-ogy medical advances today are beyond their reach. It would, therefore, be foolhardy to place too much store by this type of cloning, even if it does become scientifically feasible and even if a limited number of people can genuinely benefit from it.

This leaves the far larger question of the reproductive cloning of oneself. The experience of the scientist in the parable is a grim reminder that the reality will probably turn out to be very differ-ent from the naive idealism of many who have written about reproductive cloning over the past few years. The photocopying image so beloved of writers and journalists bears no relation to the way in which biology operates. Variability lies at the heart of all things biological, including human beings, and cloning is not suddenly going to put an end to that – even if it restricts variabil-ity more than we are used to.

But the even more important question is: What do we want out of life? The scientist in the parable wanted to be remembered for his great scientific achievements. There is nothing wrong with that, as long as we realize that these achievements are not nearly as momentous as most of us fondly imagine. Most of us, within twenty-five years of our deaths, will be forgotten by all except a few close family members. Our significance does not lie in the future; it lies in the here and now, in what we do now, how we treat others, and the ways in which we live our lives for others. Our sacrificial living in the present is of infinitely greater significance than what people may or may not remember of our achievements. Even if our achievements have a good influence on those in the future, it is what those achievements are able to do that is important, not the name of the person responsible for them.

This helps to put in perspective one of the grand delusions about cloning. Even if we were to clone ourselves so that our clone lived in the next generation, we would be just as dead and long forgotten as we are in the absence of cloning. Our clone in the next generation would be precisely that, another person with their own challenges and responsibilities. They would be themselves, and not us. To expect people to remember us, rather than them, fifty or sixty years hence, is to deceive ourselves. It is also to do a grave disservice to those who come after us, regardless of how they have been brought into existence. The world of the future will be their world, not ours, in exactly the same way as it is now the world of our children and grandchildren.

What this story tells us is that cloning will probably prove far less beneficial to those who want to be cloned for egotistical reasons than is generally thought. The story is a salutary one for individuals, but what about societies? Would the character of a particular society make a difference to the cloning carried out in it?

A second salutary story

Cloning is generally discussed in a social vacuum, because it is discussed in terms of individuals and not of societies. What I want to consider in this second story is the close relationship between cloning and its implications, and the nature of the society into which it is introduced. What I want to show is that the goals of cloning will vary depending upon the dominant social philosophy of the society concerned. Imagine the following:

Society D is very conservative and abides by a strict moral code based upon monogamous marriage. Divorce is forbidden and abortion rarely takes place. Cloning is accepted by this society, although only within strict boundaries. Human reproductive cloning is used to enable a few infertile couples to have children of their own, but all these couples must be legally married. Cloning is forbidden for single people, and ego cloning is frowned upon since the welfare of the resulting children (clones) may be jeopardized. Therapeutic cloning is also allowed, although nuclei can never be taken from human embryos – they can only be taken from adult cells, and enormous efforts are made to ensure that viable embryos are never produced as part of the production of tissues. Inevitably, knife-edge decisions are being taken, and the purists within the society are not satisfied. Nevertheless, the boundaries are fairly strictly adhered to.

Society E is far more liberal, in that none of these strictures is in place, and human reproductive cloning can be used to allow anyone to have a child, regardless of marital status, age, or motive for the cloning. 'Complete freedom' is the watch-cry of this society, and reproductive freedom is the order of the day. When it comes to therapeutic cloning, clinical efficiency is all important. Whatever will advance this is accepted, regardless of whether the nuclei come from embryos or adults. Even the embryos can be obtained from any available source, and most of them are manufactured specifically for this purpose. No concerns are expressed about producing embryos as a means of producing tissues. Whatever will benefit the prospective patient is accepted.

These societies are extreme illustrations of the radically different ways in which the same technique can be used to promote different goals. There is overlap between the two, and yet the consequences for the respective societies will probably be dramatically different. The differences lie in the societies themselves, and in their prevailing attitudes. Society D is one version of a Christian society (although I do not mean to suggest that this is the only way in which a society guided by Christian principles would operate), whereas society E is closer to the attitudes of what one would expect of scientific naturalism (again, this is not inevitable, but it is possible).

Of these two models, society E characterizes the western world at present, and so may provide a provocative clue about how cloning could operate in some future society. If this the case, does it introduce serious concerns for our analysis of cloning?

Scientific naturalism and cloning

In attempting to assess the impact of scientific naturalism on cloning, we should first examine scientific naturalism, a philosophy that leaves little or no room for God. This can be readily illustrated by reference to a number of writers.

Around the time I was a student in London one of the best-known English scientists was Sir Julian Huxley, who wrote a great deal about science and religion. In the late 1960s he wrote a book called *Religion without Revelation*, in which he argued for a religion without God. For him, 'the god hypothesis has ceased to be scientifically tenable, has lost its explanatory value and is becoming an intellectual and moral burden to our thought'. What we needed, according to Huxley, was a religion that would 'promote further evolutionary improvement and [to] realize new possibilities'.[1] In his view, evolution had replaced the God of Christianity and Judaism.

Slightly later, in 1970, Jacques Monod, one of the founders of molecular biology and a Nobel Prizewinner, wrote a bleak book

---

[1] J. Huxley, *Religion without Revelation*, 4.

entitled *Chance and Necessity.* Working from the basis that human beings are accidents based on chance, he concluded that 'man at last knows he is alone in the unfeeling immensity of the universe, out of which he emerged only by chance. Neither his destiny nor his duty have been written down. The kingdom above or the darkness below: it is for him to choose'.[2] Having totally rejected any form of the Christian God, the only remaining option for humans is one of 'total solitude and fundamental isolation' in the universe. The future depends entirely on humans themselves and on their scientific abilities.

Carl Sagan in *Cosmos*, his very influential 1980 TV series and book, commenced with these words: 'The Cosmos is all that is or ever was or ever will be.' He concluded by stating, 'Our loyalties are to the species and the planet. We speak for Earth. Our obligation to survive is owed not just to ourselves but also to that Cosmos, ancient and vast, from which we spring.'[3] Sagan always writes cosmos with a capital C and earth with a capital E. For him there is nothing else. Whenever he mentions religious ideas, it is to dismiss them as superstitious and wrong. All there is, is science and the Cosmos. He appreciates the wonder of the universe, but for him it is the beginning and end of existence. For him a universe that is infinitely old requires no Creator; the cosmos has replaced God.

Richard Dawkins, the prolific science writer and evangelist for atheism, wrote in one of his earlier books, *The Blind Watchmaker*, 'Natural selection, the blind unconscious automatic process which Darwin discovered, and which we know is the explanation for the existence and apparent purposeful form of all life, has no purpose in mind. It has no mind and no mind's eye. It does not plan for the future. It has no vision, no foresight, no sight at all. If it can be said to play the role of watchmaker in nature, it is the *blind* watchmaker.'[4] For Dawkins, natural selection replaces God, who becomes superfluous – bringing God into

---

[2] J. Monod, *Change and Necessity*, 167.

[3] C. Sagan, *Cosmos*, 345.

[4] R. Dawkins, *The Blind Watchmaker*, 5.

the picture complicates everything. Nevertheless, he concedes that his view of the world is a cold and bleak one, lacking any moral direction.

Francis Crick, best known for his contribution to unravelling the structure of DNA, wrote a book in 1994 entitled *The Astonishing Hypothesis: The Scientific Search for the Soul*. In introducing this he wrote, 'The Astonishing Hypothesis is that "You", your joys and your sorrows, your memories and your ambitions, your sense of identity and free will, are in fact no more than the behaviour of a vast assembly of nerve cells and their associated molecules'.[5] Once again, what emerges is bleakness.

For these scientists there is no room for God, because evolution has become the explanatory mechanism for everything. Whatever meaning and worth humans have is measured solely by an evolutionary yardstick. The fulcrum of the universe has been shifted, and the conclusions evolutionary naturalism reaches are diametrically opposed to the Christian view. God has been replaced by a process directly opposed to him. In stating that the universe is purposeless, and that there is no hope except that which humans can manufacture for themselves, evolution has assumed its own religious authority (in the form of evolutionary naturalism).

This is the environment of most societies within which cloning will be launched. It is an environment struggling to find meaning and purpose in life, the only pointers being provided by science in general, and evolution in particular. Unfortunately, neither has proved a reliable guide for deciding how modern technology is to be developed. Driven by the technological imperative, humans are producing a novel world that revolves solely around human expectations and that is being modified increasingly by human constructions. In such a world there are numerous pressures directed towards the enhancement of human abilities, since this is seen as the only way forward within a human-centred framework. New insights and concepts can only come from more 'advanced' humans, that is, *culturally* more evolved. Hence, the

---

[5] F. Crick, *The Astonishing Hypothesis*, 3.

well-known emphasis in the literature on enhancement, particularly in the areas of intelligence, although sporting prowess and beauty are not far behind. The idealism of these hopes stems from their humanistic origins, with science as the driving force behind this form of humanism.

The dangers of cloning (especially human reproductive cloning) are to be found at this point, as the enhancement is ideologically, not therapeutically, driven. Since humans are being viewed as nothing but machines to be tampered with and improved, it is entirely fitting that something like cloning should be used in this way. The machine analogy is, of course, a very old one, and indeed an antiquated one, and yet it rears its head repeatedly in societies dominated by scientific naturalism. It is hardly surprising that critics of the artificial reproductive technologies, let alone cloning, condemn these procedures because of the manner in which children appear to be manufactured, that is, produced to order. This may or may not be a fair criticism of the techniques as a whole, but unless societies are exceedingly careful, child-manufacture is a possible end result of such forays into the reproductive area.

Unless this sounds unduly futuristic, consider the following real-life case, that hit the headlines in October 2000. A Colorado couple used genetic tests to create a test-tube baby that would have the exact type of cells needed to save their six-year-old daughter. The case represents the first time a couple is known to have screened their embryos before implanting one in the mother's uterus for the purpose of saving the life of the sibling. Adam, the resulting baby, was born in Denver. Doctors collected cells from his umbilical cord, and a month later infused them into his sister Molly's circulatory system.

The easy response to this case is to dismiss it as unethical and unworthy of loving parents. And yet, as with so many of these cases, the situation refuses to be this black and white. While there is no doubt it gives the distinct impression of treating the newborn baby in an instrumental fashion, it also provided a 'treatment' for the existing child. Without this sequence of events, the six-year-old would have died of Fanconi anaemia, a fatal inherited bone marrow deficiency. Did this outcome justify 'manufacturing' another child to serve as the life-saver? Is choosing the traits of one's child in this manner (for this or some comparable reason) justified? Can it ever be justified?

Many people intuitively feel there is far too much control involved in actions of this nature. But why should control be bad? Is it possible to exert too much control? I have already touched on the ambivalence of control – without it there would be no technology; it can be abused, but it also makes possible the defeat of disease and illness. The other side of control in this instance is to ask whether a child like Adam can be loved? By controlling the reproductive process do we automatically cease to love the product?

While questions like these are new ones, they force us to confront the motives people have for bringing children into the world. Indeed, are our motives important as far as the new child is concerned, as long as the new child (the aptly named Adam in this instance) is loved deeply? To assert that the Adams of this world can never be loved is unjustified, however much we disagree with the processes used. What is more important is to ask whether the environment within which procedures like this are being employed is inimical to the welfare of any resulting children. Does scientific naturalism have anything within it to protect them and to prevent societies from grossly misusing cloning and other biomedical procedures? What sort of ethical guidelines are required?

The surprising rejection of cloning

If control is as crucial to scientific naturalism as I have suggested, one might anticipate that cloning would be welcomed in our societies today. One would expect a materialist guiding philosophy to find cloning eminently congenial, since any form of manipulation that allows humans to be the manipulators of their own destiny should be exceedingly attractive. And yet, this may not be the inevitable way ahead. It is in precisely the same societies that there has been such an outcry against human reproductive cloning (and to a lesser extent, against human therapeutic cloning). Why is this? Why should such repugnance be felt? Where does this repugnance come from?

We have already seen in Chapter 3 that the arguments against cloning are many and varied, stretching from the 'yuk' reaction at one end to concerns over human dignity at the other. We need not agree with all of the arguments to realize that they stem from a fear that the human person would be placed at peril by the advent of cloning. There remains a strong perception that to remove someone's individuality (or even appear to do so) is to jeopardize the essence of the person. This, however, is simply part of a far more general reaction against genetic engineering, the manipulation of human beings. These perceptions sit uneasily alongside the thrusts of scientific naturalism, and seem to suggest that the lack of any convincing ethical principles emanating from it have left a vacuum when it comes to assessing something as dramatic as human cloning.

We are left in an uneasy situation. Proponents of scientific naturalism see no problems with human cloning in any of its forms, which is hardly surprising, since scientific naturalism suggests that science can explain everything; it is the only true source of knowledge. But this claims far too much for science, because scientific naturalism cannot itself be demonstrated scientifically, any more than Christian beliefs can be demonstrated scientifically. That is not the sort of thing that science can do.

Science excludes a great deal from its methods. For example, scientific descriptions do not help us to understand the joy of beautiful music, the wonder of a newborn baby, the exhilaration of passing an exam, or the depths of despair at a personal tragedy. If you want to learn more about love, beauty, poetry, art, friendship or moral judgements, you do not use the methods of science. It is true that brain waves and hormonal levels can be measured in all these instances, but measurements are quite different from the experiences themselves. A scientific approach is not the appropriate one in any of these instances. In the same way, science does not help us understand God, or sacrifice for a higher cause, or commitment to religious ideals. Science is of immense value, but it is not the only way to understand the world in which we live, let alone the meaning of human existence.

Think about ethics. We desperately need ethical guidelines to help us through a morass of difficult situations, especially in modern medicine. And yet scientific naturalism seems to deprive us of ethics even though numerous attempts have been made over many years to demonstrate that this is not the case. For instance, evolutionary naturalism attempts to use evolutionary explanations to explain all aspects of human behaviour. The arguments are difficult to follow, but they assume that all ethical decision-making can be explained in biological terms. Thus morality becomes an innate biological drive derived from our genetic inheritance; in other words, moral values are innately natural. But why we may ask should one set of urges be more moral than another? There are also scientific problems with this sort of explanation, since the genetic basis of moral behaviour is far from clear: morality is far more likely to be culturally inherited.

This leaves us with a predicament, since science by itself will provide no insights into whether clones are to be produced, or whether cloned tissues are to be employed in research and therapy. It fails to enunciate a moral basis for questions like these. Clones can be produced, but should they be? Scientific naturalism struggles at this point, and has not proved convincing when confronted by such detailed questions. Grandiose overconfidence in the potential of science is the order of the day. We are either informed that we can understand our origins and so are in a position to design our future, or merely that it might be interesting to clone ourselves. Either way, we are given the impression that nature is infinitely malleable and that the possibilities open to science are equally infinite. This is to give a gravely misleading impression of the current state of genetic science, since many of our hopes will not materialize. It is also unwise to place too much store by any currently favoured technology, which will be surpassed and will fail to meet up to excessive expectations.

Furthermore, humans must beware of alienating themselves from the system on which they are working, whether this be the environment or their own bodies – we do not stand over against either the environment or our bodies, as we are intricately intertwined with our environment, and our bodies are ourselves. When we manipulate either of these we manipulate something with a direct effect on what we are and how we live; we are not isolated observers, but are inseparable from the physical world.

If we fail to appreciate the limitations of the technology we are employing, and our own vulnerability within the physical world, we shall come to believe that social problems have physical solutions. Time and again, we have fallen into this trap, expecting drugs, pills and potions to remedy ills brought about by social malaises and inequities. The genetic realm introduces even greater pitfalls, if we expect cloning to replace lost children or provide a temporal form of immortality. Any such expectations are based on false expectations of what science can do for us, and if this is where scientific naturalism takes us we should ruthlessly reveal its bankruptcy.

Genetics has huge potential in rectifying specific conditions that diminish ordinary people. This is where we should look to it for assistance and where we should be grateful for the many advances discussed in this book. We should be grateful for these advances, whether or not we are Christians. On the other hand, if genetics is expected to solve all our problems and transform human nature, it has assumed the mantle of secular redeemer, but a mantle that will destroy rather than redeem. We lack the power to alter everything.

Perhaps this is why many ordinary people are afraid of human reproductive cloning. Both it and other genetic ventures, are presented (perhaps inadvertently) in these overbearing terms. They will accomplish too much; they will transform all that we know and experience; they make us feel vulnerable and small. All too readily they give the impression that the world we know is about to be turned upside down, and there is nothing we can do about it. We are our genes, and our genes are amenable to being tampered with. Such genetic determinism may or may not be intended, but it lies just beneath the surface, and we – humans – are at the mercy of the gene manipulators. As will have become obvious throughout the course of this book, I have no sympathy with emphases of this type, nor with the fear of genetics. The problem is that triumphant scientific naturalism lends itself to these emphases, and they divert attention away from the virtues of genetics, including the potential virtues of some forms of cloning.

It would be sad indeed if the baby were to be thrown out with the bath water: the possibilities of genetic science with the grave disadvantages of genetic determinism and scientific naturalism. And yet this could well happen, since there is a widespread feeling that science and technology have failed to deliver the goods. For many outside science, the drawbacks of science outweigh any virtues it may possess. Antipathy caused by the depersonalization of modern medicine, the pollution of the environment, and the commercialism of university science, leads inevitably to a deep repugnance at the threat posed to human embryos by scientific research and therefore to an equally virulent rejection of cloning in all its guises. No wonder the ordinary public has grave reservations about any form of genetic manipulation.

Scientific naturalism has signally failed the modern world of genetic manipulation. The rationalist-materialist-reductionist outlook cannot supply satisfactory answers to today's urgent questions in the genetic realm let alone in the more narrowly focused area of cloning. But is there a better way? Can Christian thinking provide any assistance, or is it just as stultified, but for different reasons?

Christian signposts: the image of God

If scientific naturalism is inadequate, how might a Christian approach help out? To probe this we have to begin with God as Creator, and with the fundamental assertion that God is the Creator of everything that exists (Gen. 1:1–5; Ps. 8:3–4; 100:3; Acts 17:24–5).

This tells us in the first place that God is basic to everything – inanimate matter, the living world, human beings; he is responsible for bringing all these into existence. Not only this; the God who has created us is a personal God. When we recognize this, we begin to see that the universe is imbued with purpose, a purpose that enables human beings to find meaning in the world. This is something we can never overemphasize, because without meaning an impersonal world soon becomes a hostile and forbidding place. As people created by a personal God, we are not the end products of random, purposeless processes. It is God who is the centre of life, and we have meaning as people because of this. If this is the case, humans themselves have no authority to treat other humans in impersonal ways, to treat them as though they are nothing more than the impersonal end products of factory-like processes. This does not place all forms of cloning out of court, but it provides a powerful framework for considering what is or is not acceptable.

Second, this personal God is close to us as well as over us. It is easy to think of a Creator as someone who is remote – the Creator who is 'out there', who set the machine in motion and has now left it to run its course. That is to view God as the cosmic mechanic, a view foreign to a Christian stance. For Christians, God is actively involved in keeping the world going; he is interested in human welfare; he is close to us and is concerned about us. If you like, he is the cosmic artist. For Christians, the Creator is both 'out there', and alongside us through the events of everyday living. If this applies to the Creator it should also apply to humans as those with responsibility for bringing others into existence; these new creations are like us, are one with us, and bear the same marks as us. We are not above them simply because we have used our technological creativity to give them life. Like us, their life is derived ultimately from God and not from us. We are no more their creators than is a couple who give birth to a child by following the most natural of processes.

Third, Christians recognize a sharp distinction between the Creator and the created, between God himself and all else that depends upon him for its existence and sustenance. This means that nature, the creation, can be known and controlled. It can be treated with respect and seriousness because it is God's handiwork. It can be enjoyed, because it is no longer at the mercy of the vagaries of malevolent and capricious gods, or even of impersonal forces. Cloning at its best (and this will generally mean therapeutic cloning) could illustrate this sort of control, as long as it is not an exercise in human bravado. In explicit Christian terms, this signifies dependence upon God.

What is important here is the ultimate fact that God created, that he is involved in his creation, and that he deals with humanity in mercy and love. This approach takes us to the heart of Christian thinking. Why value human life and human beings? Why be concerned about the poor, the disadvantaged and clones? Christians start with God as Creator, with God's concern for his world, and with our dependence upon him and his goodness.

We are all made in the image of God, no matter how we came into being – whether we were conceived in love or in lust, whether we were wanted or not, whether we were fertilized naturally or artificially, and even in the future if we were to be created by cloning. All humans image God, and hence are to be treated as beings deserving of dignity and fairness, and are to be given the opportunity to be themselves.

It is all too easy to treat some people or some groups of people as subhuman, or at least as of somewhat lesser status and importance than everyone else. We do this all the time, and it is these attitudes that lead to the biggest problems facing our world: ethnic groups who are disparaged, groups with medical problems who are looked upon as second-class citizens, indigenous groups in all societies who are disadvantaged in numerous ways throughout their lives. Whenever this happens, we are implicitly judging some people as of little worth, which God never does. In other words, this is not a problem that will one day emerge because of how clones are treated; it is a problem we live with all the time because our horizons are far more restricted than are God's.

But if this is the case, why clone in the first place? Why should we as societies be expected to place a high value on people who are different from us, if they were brought into the world to be exactly the same as some of us? As we have seen previously, the mere asking of this question highlights the problematic nature of some forms of cloning. Once society allows this to happen for purely egotistical reasons, it will expect to treat these people differently.

This was well brought out in the film *Gattaca*, which was set in a world of highly sophisticated genetic technology. The major problems there were with social attitudes, since those who were apparently second–rate on a genetic scale of values were treated as second rate by that society. The end result was that a form of genetic determinism ruled the society, and inequality was rampant. What was fascinating about the film was that certain individuals, the 'invalids', the second-rate citizens, refused to accept their lowly status and subtly demonstrated that they were far more than their genes. This is a profoundly Christian emphasis that points to the importance of wholeness and integrity in our lives, since it is these attributes that mirror what we are in the sight of God.

Christians will want to emphasize the idea of servanthood (Mark 10:41–5). Christ's coming to earth, and then the manner in which he lived and ultimately died, were dominated by this one emphasis, that he came to serve others. In precisely the same way, those who follow him are to be set apart from others by the quality and character of their service of others. Christians are to serve others, regardless of how these others were conceived or of any of their other characteristics. Christians are to be like Christ, not lording it over others, whether these be clones or anyone else. They are to serve others, and are never to expect others to treat them as superior on any grounds whatsoever. We are never to bring others into the world so that they can dance to our tune, and this includes perfectly ordinary and straightforward children, let alone clones. Cloning, therefore, is not a quick way to the production of a class of slaves. If human clones ever exist, they should be served by others, while they themselves should live out their lives in a spirit of servanthood.

Christian signposts: neither cloned nor fertilized

Diversity is important, both within society at large and within the church. Even were clones to emerge as exemplary citizens, the danger would be that the diversity of human experience would have been downgraded. The trouble even now is that we want everyone to be like us. Life would be so much easier if others thought like us, dressed like us, behaved like us, and had the same aspirations as us. Our temptation is to want churches to be full of similar people, who believe the same things even down to the minutiae, have the same attitudes, and act in the same ways. But this is an appalling heresy, because God has made us different, which is why the picture of the church as the body of Christ is so powerful (1 Cor. 12). We all have our respective contributions to make to this functioning body, and if these different contributions are not forthcoming the body will be unable to function properly.

In biological terms, ordinary genetic inheritance ensures that children have a mix of their parents' characteristics. There are many reasons for this biologically, but in Christian terms part of the reasoning is that God deals with us as individuals; we are unique creations who mirror God in our own unique ways. God loves us as individuals, as the different characters we all are. He loves us for what we are, and for what we can bring to his world, regardless of our intellectual and manual abilities, or lack of them. We are loved by God simply because we are loved by God. Sadly we spend so much of our time trying to downplay this, being afraid of the challenges and responsibilities this bestows upon us. Clones, therefore, appear to be an anomaly, since we should not strive for sameness just for its own sake. On the other hand, should human reproductive cloning eventuate we will be able to cope with it, since we already cope with identical twins, let alone identical triplets.

How would we react if confronted by a clone? From a Christian angle, we ought to respond exactly as we should to anyone else: with acceptance and a recognition of who they are before God. Surely God would call clones in exactly the same way as he calls ordinary people who started off life as fertilized embryos.

We are all one in Christ Jesus: 'There is neither Jew nor Greek, slave nor free, male nor female, for you are all one in Christ Jesus' (Gal. 3:28); and we can add that there is neither black nor white, Asian nor Caucasian, clone nor fertilized. In Christ, distinctions like these disappear. Although they still exist at a social level, they are of no importance when we look at each other in Christ. This has been revolutionary teaching throughout the past two thousand years, and it applies just as powerfully in the twenty-first century. And what applies within the church should apply in society at large: there is an equality between individuals that we dare not overlook, regardless of what people are like in the present, and regardless of how they commenced their lives.

All in the church are one in Christ, whoever they are. Christ loves us regardless of what we bring to him. It is faith that is central, faith in his redeeming work on the cross. Should clones ever be brought into existence, the same will be true for them. This is our hope, and it would be their hope. Clones will be much more like us than they will be like the androids of science fiction. They will be God's creations just as we are, and will stand before him as we do.

This is brought out delightfully by the story of Jesus' encounter with Nicodemus, a sterling and upright leader of the Jews, who wanted to clarify what Jesus was teaching. It was in response to his queries that Jesus emphasized the need to be 'born again'. If Nicodemus wanted to enter the kingdom of God, it was not enough for him to be a worthy religious leader, nor did he have to do anything as dramatic as enter a second time into his mother's womb (John 3:1–8). Nicodemus had to learn that the new birth has nothing to do with a biological process. Christians cannot be made biologically, any more than they can be made socially. Entering the kingdom of God has nothing to do with cloning; after all, identical twins can have quite different relationships to Christ.

Clones would be far more ordinary than we often imagine, and they would be in need of God's love and mercy just like everyone else. Not only this, they would be human beings created in the image of God, rather than in the approximate image of another human being. But this is just like all of us. Some of our parents may have fostered the unfortunate illusion that we are such delightful individuals because we are like them (who by definition are delightful!). On the other hand, some parents do everything to ensure that their children will be better educated or have more opportunities than they had, with the intention that they will end up as better versions of themselves. And then, inevitably, some parents end up disillusioned because little Johnny or little Mary is not what they had imagined; Johnny and Mary are different because, for better or worse, they are themselves. And so, even if in a science fiction future there was a Nicodemus who was a clone, he would still need to be born again, that is, born from above, as did the Nicodemus of old (John 3:16).

Another helpful pointer is provided by the way in which Jesus responded to children (Matt. 18:1–5). He welcomed them because of what they are; he used them as a picture of humility, and even suggested that whoever welcomes children welcomes Jesus himself. Children are not to be seen as nuisances or hindrances to the lives of adults, who live in some real world uncluttered by the noise and mess of children. The lives of adults are to take into account the needs and weaknesses and demands of children. They are pictures of the sort of humility that is to characterize the attitudes of the followers of Jesus, indeed the attitudes of everyone. If human clones ever exist, they are to be welcomed as children are to be welcomed, and are to be accepted as ordinary people with ordinary needs and ordinary expectations.

Cloning and God's providence

But we are still left with nagging questions. Are we going too far? Is modern biological science out of control? Is God in it, or has he left us to our own devices, so that we shall eventually destroy ourselves?

Many, including many Christians, think this is the case. However, if we do respond in this way, we all too readily overlook God's providence – his constant concern for his creation. As we take account of that, we begin to see that his faithfulness will not desert us, and that he will not allow us to abrogate what is rightfully his. We tinker with human life, but we do not create new human life in some dramatic new way. There is much we do not understand scientifically, and probably never will. We personally may be unhappy about the directions taken by some scientific research, and yet we are still functioning within limits set by God. There is no way in which humans can become gods, however much they may sometimes try. Our abilities are simply those that reflect what we are as creatures made in the image of God. Once we take this as our foundation we shall look at the world rather differently – through the eyes of faith and not through the eyes of fear.

The apostle Paul, in writing to the Christians in Rome, summed up much of this so nicely. As we look forward with the eyes of faith we look forward to a time when 'the creation itself will be set free from its bondage to decay and will obtain the freedom of the glory of the children of God. We know that the whole creation has been groaning in labour pains until now, and not only the creation, but we ourselves, who have the first fruits of the Spirit, groan inwardly while we wait for adoption, the redemption of our bodies' (Rom. 8:21–3). 'What then are we to say about these things? If God is for us, who is against us? He who did not withhold his own Son, but gave him up for all of us, will he not with him also give us everything else?' (Rom. 8:31–2).

God is sovereign, acting in ways far beyond our comprehension. To become depressed at what we see, and conclude that God is being shut out of the picture, simply tells us that our view of him is a tragically small one. This is not to say that we glibly accept everything that happens or could happen in science or in anything else for that matter. There was a time when theological debates raged around whether or not to administer anaesthetics to women in labour, since some viewed this as doing something of which God did not approve (see Gen. 3:16). I doubt whether any would now see this as a crucial theological question that reflects our faithfulness or otherwise to the early chapters of Genesis. Perhaps cloning, rightly used, will be seen in the same light in sixty or seventy years' time.

In St Giles' Cathedral in Edinburgh, one of the wall plaques stands out. It thanks God for the discovery of anaesthesia by James Stewart Young in 1836. Other plaques are more conventional as they praise God or simply remember some outstanding churchman or theologian. There is nothing wrong with such sentiments, but they vastly outnumber those that remember a scientific discovery or medical advance. As I stood and contemplated the James Stewart Young plaque recently, I wondered whether a similar plaque would one day grace that same cathedral, thanking God for the contributions of Ian Wilmut, working just outside Edinburgh, in opening the way to cloning.

For some any such a thought is anathema. How can God possibly be thanked for such a development? But why not? As our successors look back at cloning and at what it may one day have achieved for human welfare, they may well feel that this is a work of God. God is in control, and his purposes are so far above ours. We need to remember this when tempted to think that humans can totally alter the way the world functions and equally when we fear that God has lost out to scientific achievements. God's providence helps us achieve a balance between foolish arrogance on the one hand, and faithless temerity on the other.

What I have been saying about clones and cloning challenges us to ask how Christianity influences our thinking and attitudes across all areas of our lives. My response is along the following lines.

First, Christianity sets the direction for our thinking and actions on issues like cloning, even if it is not generally a simple 'yes/no' or 'right/wrong' answer. Nevertheless, it should always inform the way in which we approach matters, from cloning at one end to politics at the other, with buying a house, a car or a TV set somewhere in the middle. It will not tell us to buy a Toyota rather than a Vauxhall or anything like that, but it will give us a context and a reminder of the important priorities within which to make a decision.

Second, Christians are to search the Bible for whatever helpful pointers can be found. The sorts of issues dealt with in this book do not lend themselves to any specific answers, but there are general signposts. We are not to despair at the complexity of some of the issues surrounding us, especially in scientific areas. We are to face them squarely, seek the assistance of others who have thought more about these particular matters, and seek the direction of the Holy Spirit, for our actions, our thinking, and our own response.

Third, society has been changed dramatically by many forms of technology, and Christian standards have been threatened in many ways. Technologies like those in the reproductive area have to be put to good ends, although different social perspectives have made this task a daunting one. But all is not lost. Life may be easier without technologies like cloning (even of the therapeutic variety), and yet if they can be used for good they have a place within the armamentarium of contemporary health services.

These responses can be interpreted as individualistic ones, in that they seek to help us as individuals in our assessment of technologies. Is there a far more encompassing Christian viewpoint, in the sense that Christians as a whole should respond en masse in some way or other? For some this is the case. For them, there is a Christian position on an issue like cloning, and it is to oppose cloning of any description. According to this perspective, cloning is the antithesis of Christian aspirations, because the way in which it brings children into the world is far too instrumental and manipulative. When children are not being manipulated, human embryos are. Either way is a negation of Christian attitudes. My argument has been that this conclusion is not an inevitable outcome of Christian thinking. I am deeply sympathetic towards it, but for me Christian thinking directs our attention at the specific applications rather than at the general approach. It forces us to weigh up each new development and proposal, and assess each individual case. It stresses the importance of our motives, the moral and spiritual significance of the way we view and treat children (whether cloned or fertilized), and it reminds us that we are humbly to confess the limitations and inadequacies of all technological procedures.

Humour, clones and clowns

One of the problems with modern science, and with the ethics that accompany it, is that we take ourselves too seriously. We come to think that we can do more than we really can, and that we really do hold the world in our hands, or at least the destiny of limitless numbers of people in our hands. All too readily we come to think of ourselves as omnipotent, able to bring perfect life into being, able to bring to an end imperfect life, and able to ward off death indefinitely. All are dangerous illusions. No matter how great our abilities, they need to be balanced by humility; only in this way will they be directed to ends aimed at improving the welfare of as many as possible. In discussing suffering and ways of coping with death, a German Protestant ethicist, Udo Schlaudraff, has written, 'The job of ethical thinking in this field is to discern the difference between hardship which is inevitable and that which is not because it is manmade.'[6] He then looks to Psalm 90 for a perspective that provides a realistic view of ourselves and our place in God's world:.

> Lord, you have been our dwelling-place
> in all generations.
> Before the mountains were brought forth,
> or ever you had formed the earth and the world,
> from everlasting to everlasting you are God ...
> For all our days pass away under your wrath;
> our years come to an end like a sigh.
> The days of our life are seventy years,
> or perhaps eighty, if we are strong ...
> So teach us to count our days
> that we may gain a wise heart. (Ps. 90:1–2, 9–10, 12, NRSV)

It is in seeking this realistic balance that we need humour. James Houston has dealt with this at some length in his book *I Believe*

---

[6] U. Schlaudraff, 'How to Become an Ethicist? A Narrative Reflection', 15.

in the Creator. Referring, for instance, to Psalm 2:4 with its reference to God sitting in the heavens and laughing, he sees God as a cosmic and compassionate comedian. For Houston, humour tells us something about our humanity, God's grace, and the careful ordering of God's world with its congruities rather than chaos (Is. 40:12–14; 45:18–19; Ps. 65:6–7). These provide the background for our approach to the incongruities that touch all our lives. How do we cope when things go wrong, when our vast plans come to nought, and when our brilliance seems all too inadequate? The paths along which we so often go are those of despair, cynicism, invective and sarcasm. But there is an alternative – humour. Houston comments, 'Satire, invective and sarcasm will have its victims, irony will seek its own magic circle, but true humour sees humanity bound together in its incongruities'.[7]

Like the clown, we are not always to take ourselves too seriously. We are to place our immaculate plans in a much broader context. But this can only be done if we eschew arrogance and refuse to see ourselves as the centre of all wisdom. One way of doing this is to seek assistance in comedy, which is one means of recognizing the false idols of the world and hence of deflating our pretensions. There is an urgent need for this in technological societies, which, as we have seen, tend to take their abilities with deadly seriousness. After all, how often do we see gargoyles on downtown skyscrapers, let alone in scientific laboratories? We need to be able to laugh at our overweening pretensions and misguided designs. Whenever we think we can 'cure' death, or create babies in our own image, we need to step back and laugh at the comic situation created by our pretensions. If we are unable to do this, we will weep and despair when we are let down, as most surely we will be.

There is no harm in acknowledging and celebrating the immensity of some of our achievements, since we should be grateful for these. But accompanying each celebration there should be a counterbalance, an awareness that we cannot

---

[7] J. Houston, *I Believe in the Creator*, 221.

achieve everything. And for that we should be grateful, because if we could achieve everything (or at least think we could achieve everything), we would soon find that such hubris would prove fatal.

For Houston, the essence of comedy is discrepancy. He comments:

> There is also discrepancy when man sees himself as his own master and creator, when the Creator is King of the universe. Cosmic catharsis gives man the fleeting awareness of his finitude, so while in tragedy there is suffering and struggle, in comedy there is ultimate hope and transcendence. The comic too, is the refusal to accept the *status quo*, unmasking human pretensions ... The Christian goes about the world, tongue in cheek, as God's clown, knowing that the mask he wears on earth will one day become a real face in heaven.[8]

Humour like this points to the transitoriness of life on earth, emphasizing that our lives are temporal, that we are mortal, that we will not live for ever and should not expect to do so. From the Christian perspective it also reminds us that present existence and present experiences are not all there is. We have been created by God who sustains and upholds us, and to whom we will one day be accountable. Our present life on earth is indeed a journey – it is not the destination. We are strangers passing through, and while we take this existence and our responsibilities very seriously indeed, the theme of being strangers colours very much what we are and how we live.

Another Christian emphasis is one we have already encountered: that of learning to be childlike, to be innocent, accepting what God has to offer, and being thankful for his many gifts. Gratitude is closely bound up in the childlike spirit, as children look to their parents for protection and nurture. In Christian terms, gratitude of this order should characterize us as we look to God, our heavenly parent, to look after us in these same ways. Humour is closely involved in being like little children who simply enjoy life and what it has to offer. In his parables, as he

---

[8] J. Houston, *I Believe in the Creator*, 225.

imparted profound truths, and as he debunked the pretentious religious leaders of his day, Jesus was also capable of humour and wit (Matt. 7:7–11; 23:1–36; Luke 6:39–42). Humour is one of the most effective means we have of pricking the balloon of pomposity and self-interest: our own as well as others'.

Childlikeness is essential if we are to be able to accept our need of God's grace and mercy. But in doing this we acknowledge that human wisdom is inadequate, and that we have to laugh at its limitations. In other words, humour is needed to enjoy grace, as we learn to appreciate how much we mess things up and how great is our need of God's help. As we see the limitations of our own endeavours, we begin to see where we can go for assistance and support, and we learn to laugh at how little we are capable of. We need to be liberated from ourselves, in order to enjoy the presence of God and all he has to offer. By laughter we acknowledge the human condition, and seek the transcendent power of God.

There are incongruities all around us. We spend vast sums of money and effort in saving a few lives while recklessly putting an end to others for the sake of convenience. We look to cloning to solve numerous medical conditions in the future, while many people in one country after another are unable to benefit from the most meagre of medical treatments. The ethical spotlight is all too often directed upon only a few dilemmas, while ignoring others brought about by a lack of resources or by commercial imperialism. For those attempting to weigh up these predicaments, the temptation to become cynical and to despair is very great indeed. What hope can there possibly be when we seem so inept at controlling obvious injustice? The tragedy is that such a world has no room for comedy, dominated as it is by absurdity.

But there is a way through the absurdity, and this lies in a world-view that recognizes our ultimate dependence upon God. In him our laughter and tears can be accommodated and reconciled, as we come face to face with grace and mercy, and as we glimpse the place of suffering and hope in a world full of discordance and inexplicable happenings.

What place then for cloning? Are clones the clowns of medical technology, as the subheading of this book suggests? No, human clones should be accorded exactly the same high value as every other human, and will no more be clowns than anyone else is to be regarded as a clown. On the other hand, we should indeed laugh at the pretensions of those who think that cloning (in the guise of human reproductive cloning) is a serious way ahead for the human race. To see it as the path into some bright new dawn is to misunderstand both the science and the theology of cloning. We need to laugh at such hopeless aspirations. A comic response is required, and humour will prevent us making fools of ourselves.

Yet the possible therapeutic applications of the cloning of tissues is a far more serious venture. Here we do stand at the start of a new era: more the realm of the serious scientist and clinician than the clown – but also not without its problems and pitfalls. But even here we should recognize a place for humour. Not every person will be able to have his or her own tissue banks to provide for every emergency. Even if some do have these, a highly debatable question at present, most will not, and those who do have them will soon find that, useful as they may be in some situations, they will be useless in others. Here too humour has a place. Tissue banks are no panacea for every illness, let alone for disillusionment, dashed expectations, spoiled relationships, or a lack of hope and fulfilment.

Questions for group discussion

1. How do you react to the story of the famous scientist? How would you counsel him, or others like him?
2. Talk about the story of the two societies, D and E. Do you think the picture presented by society D is a feasible one?
3. Discuss the real-life case of Adam. Do you think that having a baby for this reason can ever be justified, and do you think Adam can be truly loved?
4. If science is unable to provide ethical directions for the way in which scientific developments are used, where can such

direction come from? What contributions can Christian thinking make?

5. Do you see a place for humour in our lives, especially when confronted by immense technological challenges?

Glossary

Blastocyst: name given to an early embryo at four to five days gestation after it reaches the cavity of the uterus; consists of a sphere of cells, with a fluid-filled cavity.

Blastomere: one cell of a blastocyst.

Blastula: the hollow ball of cells marking the end stage of cleavage during early embryonic development.

Cell cycle: an ordered sequence of events in the life of a dividing cell; composed of the M, G_1, S and G_2 stages.

Chromosomes: long thread-like associations of genes found in the nucleus of a cell; consist of DNA and protein.

Cleavage: the succession of rapid cell divisions without growth during early embryonic development that converts the zygote into a ball of cells.

Cloning: asexual reproduction in which the nucleus (and chromosomes) of an ovum is replaced with the nucleus of a somatic (body) cell of an adult. This fertilizes the ovum without the involvement of sperm.

Differentiation: the process of becoming specialized, as during embryonic development when cells take on a certain form and function and become ordered into tissues and organs.

Donor insemination (DI): artificial insemination with the sperm from a donor.

Egg: the female gamete, also referred to as an oocyte or ovum, from a woman's ovary.

Embryo: the stage of development up to eight weeks gestation in humans, by which point all the major organs have been laid down. The first two weeks after fertilization are variously referred to as pre-embryo or pre-implantation embryo.

Embryo biopsy: removal of one cell at the four- or eight-cell stage, in order to test it for genetic and chromosomal abnormalities; a whole individual can develop from the remaining cells.

Enhancement genetic engineering: use of techniques to manipulate the genetic information of an organism in order to improve its characteristics rather than to correct deficiencies.

Enucleated egg: removal of the nucleus from an egg (oocyte), as the prelude to cloning.

Eugenics: study of methods of improving the quality of the human race by breeding and genetic manipulation; the subject of intense debate since the late nineteenth century.

Fertilization: conventionally considered to be the act of rendering gametes fertile or capable of further development; begins with contact between spermatozoon and ovum, leading to their fusion, which stimulates the completion of ovum maturation.

Fibroblast: a type of cell found in connective tissue that secretes the protein ingredients of extracellular fibres.

Fetus: the developing human being from the end of the eighth week of gestation until birth.

Gamete: the mature male or female sex cell.

Gene: the biological unit of heredity; a unit of DNA in a chromosome, controlling the formation of a single protein.

Gene therapy: the replacement of a gene responsible for a disease like cystic fibrosis, by a (normal) gene in an attempt to remove that disease from the individual; this may be carried out either in the embryo or in the individual after birth.

Genetic engineering: the manipulation of genetic information in an embryo in order to control the characteristics of the future individual; the term is frequently used in a negative, critical sense.

Genome: the entire genetic material of an organism; includes the genetic material located in both the nucleus and the mitochondria.

Germ line cell: a sexual reproductive cell (or gamete) such as sperm and eggs.

Germ line gene therapy: the process of inserting a gene into a germ cell in order to remove a disease from the modified individual. When the latter reproduces, the modification is also present in the offspring.

Gestation: the period of development from the time of fertilization of the ovum until birth.

Human genome project (HGP): a major scientific project with the aim of producing a complete nucleotide sequence of the human genome.

Human reproductive cloning: the use of somatic cell nuclear transfer (SCNT) to produce genetically identical human beings.

Human therapeutic cloning: the use of somatic cell nuclear transfer (SCNT) to produce tissues for medical purposes rather than complete human beings.

Intracytoplasmic sperm injection (ICSI): an assisted reproductive technique used in some cases of male infertility; involves the injection of a sperm directly into the oocyte.

Implantation: the embedding of the early embryo (between six to fourteen days gestation) in the lining of the uterus (womb), so that further development of the embryo can take place.

Inner cell mass: the cluster of cells in a blastocyst that protrude into the fluid-filled cavity, and subsequently develop into the embryo proper and some of the supporting tissues; four to six days gestation.

***In vitro* fertilization (IVF):** the process of fertilizing a (human) egg with a (human) sperm *in vitro* in the laboratory and therefore outside the body of the woman. Embryo transfer may follow. The term IVF is used to cover both the fertilization and the embryo transfer.

Mitochondria: organelles in cells that serve as sites of cellular respiration; they convert energy into forms the cell can use for its various processes.

Nuclear genome: the genetic material located in the nucleus.

Oocyte: precursor of a woman's egg; often used loosely to refer to the egg.

Parthenogenesis: a form of reproduction in which females produce offspring from unfertilized eggs.

Pharming: the process by which therapeutically valuable materials such as proteins can be produced within genetically modified livestock.

Somatic cell: any cell of the body other than germ cells (egg or sperm); or any cell of an embryo, fetus, child or adult not destined to become a sperm or egg cell.

Somatic cell nuclear transfer (SCNT): the transfer of the nucleus of a somatic (body) cell of an adult into an ovum which has had its nucleus removed; also known as cloning.

Stem cells: undifferentiated cells which can divide indefinitely, and in some cases are capable of forming any cell type in the body.

Totipotent: referring to embryonic cells that retain the potential to form all parts of an organism.

Uterus (womb): hollow muscular organ in the female body, in which the fertilized ovum normally becomes embedded, and in which the developing embryo and fetus are nourished.

Zygote: the diploid product of the union of the male and female gametes in conception; a fertilized egg.

Bibliography

Abate, Tom, 'The Gene Age: Two groups on verge of reading the entire human gene code', *San Fransisco Gate*, 25 April 2000

Bruce, Donald, 'A view from Edinburgh' in Ronald Cole-Turner (ed.), *Human Cloning: Religious Responses* (Louisville, KY: Westminster / John Knox Press, 1997), 1–11

Campbell, K.H.S. et al., 'Sheep Cloned by Nuclear Transfer from a Cultured Cell Line', *Nature* 380 (1996), 64–6

Center for Bioethics and Human Dignity, Public testimony before NBAC meeting in Northbrook, IL, 11 May 1999

Church of Scotland, *Cloning Animals and Humans*, General Assembly Report, May 1997

Cole-Turner, Ronald, *The New Genesis* (Louisville, KY: Westminster / John Knox Press, 1993)

—, 'At the Beginning' in idem (ed.), *Human Cloning: Religious Responses* (Louisville, KY: Westminster / John Knox Press, 1997), 119–30

Collins, Francis, 'The Human Genome Project: Tool of Atheistic Reductionism or Embodiment of the Christian Mandate to Heal?' *Science and Christian Belief* 11 (1999), 99–111

Committee of Inquiry in Human Fertilisation and Embryology, *Warnock Committee Report* (London: HMSO, 1984)

Crick, Francis, *The Astonishing Hypothesis: The Scientific Search for the Soul* (London: Simon & Schuster, 1994)

Dawkins, Richard, *The Blind Watchmaker* (Harlow: Longman, 1986)

—, *Climbing Mount Improbable* (London: Viking, 1996)

Department of Health, *Stem Cell Research: Medical Progress with Responsibility* (London: Department of Health, 2000)

Editorial, 'Hubris, Benefits and Minefields of Human Cloning', *Nature* 391 (1998), 211

Eisenberg, Leon, 'Would Cloned Humans really be like Sheep?' *New England Journal of Medicine* 340 (1999), 471–5

Elmer-Dewitt, P., 'Cloning: Where Do We Draw The Line?' *Time* (8 November 1993), 49–54

Evans, Abigail Rian, 'Saying No to Human Cloning' in Ronald Cole-Turner (ed.), *Human Cloning: Religious Responses* (Louisville, KY: Westminster / John Knox Press, 1997), 25–34

Fletcher, Joseph, 'Response to Lederberg', in Kenneth Vaux (ed.), *Who Shall Live? Medicine, Technology, Ethics* (Fortress Press: Philadelphia, 1970)

—, *The Ethics of Genetic Control* (Garden City, NY: Anchor Books, 1974), 1–218

Geron Ethics Advisory Board, 'Research with Human Embryonic Stem Cells: Ethical Considerations', *Hastings Center Report* 29 (1999), 31–6

Golombok, Susan, et al., 'Families created by the New Reproductive Technologies: Quality of Parenting and Social and Emotional Development of the Children', *Child Development* 66 (1995), 285–98

—, 'The European study of Assisted Reproduction Families: Family Functioning and Child Development', *Human Reproduction* 11 (1996), 2324–31

Grabowski, John S., 'Made Not Begotten: A Theological Analysis of Human Cloning', *Ethics and Medicine* 14 (1998), 69–72

Gurdon, J.B., and A. Colman, 'The Future of Cloning', *Nature* 402 (1999), 743–6

Hall, J.L., et al., 'Experimental Cloning of Human Polyploid Embryos using an Artificial Zona Pelucida', *American Fertility Society conjointly with the Canadian Fertility and Andrology Society*, Program Supplement, 1993 Abstracts of the Scientific and Oral Poster Sessions, Abstract 0–001, S1

Harris, John, '"Goodbye Dolly?" The Ethics of Human Cloning', *Journal of Medical Ethics* 23 (1997), 353–60

Hottois, Gilbert, 'Is Cloning the Absolute Evil?', *Human Reproduction Update* 4 (1998), 787–90

Houston, James, *I Believe in the Creator* (London: Hodder & Stoughton, 1979)

Humber, J.M., and R.F. Almeder (eds.), *Human Cloning* (Totowa, NJ: Humana Press, 1998)

Huxley, Aldous, *Brave New World* (Garden City, NY: Doubleday, Doran, 1932)

Huxley, Julian, *Religion without Revelation* (London: C.A. Watts, 1967)

Jonas, Hans, *Philosophical Essays: From Ancient Creed to Technological Man* (Englewood Cliffs, NJ: Prentice-Hall, 1974)

Jones, D. Gareth, *Manufacturing Humans* (Leicester: Inter-Varsity Press, 1987)

—, *Valuing People* (Carlisle: Paternoster Press, 1999)

—, *Speaking for the Dead* (Aldershot: Ashgate Publishers, 2000)

Kahn, Axel, 'Clone mammals ... Clone Man?', *Nature* 386 (1997), 119

Kass, Leon, *Towards a More Natural Science* (New York: The Free Press, 1985)

—, 'The Wisdom of Repugnance' in Gregory Pence (ed.), *Flesh of my Flesh: The Ethics of Cloning Humans* (Lanham, MD: Rowman & Littlefield, 1998), 13–37

King, David, 'Led by the nose into Clone Cuckoo Land', *Times Higher Education Supplement*, 21 March 1997, 11

Kolata, Gina, *Clone: The Road to Dolly, and the Path Ahead* (New York: William Morrow, 1998)

Krauthammer, C., et al., 'A Special Report on Cloning', *Time* (10 March 1997), 40–53

LaBar, Martin, 'The Pros and Cons of Human Cloning', *Thought* 59 (1984), 319–33

Lebacqz, Karen, et al. (for Geron Advisory Board), 'Research with Human Embryonic Stem Cells: Ethical Considerations', *Hastings Center Report* 29 (1999), 31–6

Lederberg, Joshua, 'Experimental Genetics and Human Evolution', *American Naturalist* 100 (1966), 519–31

McCormick, Richard A., *How Brave a New World?* (London: SCM Press, 1981)

—, 'Blastomere Separation: Some Concerns', *Hastings Center Report* 24 (1994), 14–16

McGee, Glenn, and Arthur L. Caplan, 'What's in the dish?' *Hastings Center Report* 29 (1999), 36–8

McGrath, J., and D. Stolter, 'Inability of Mouse Blastomere Nuclei Transferred to Enucleated Zygotes to Support Development *In Vitro*', *Science* 226 (1984), 1317–18

Macklin, Ruth, 'Splitting Embryos on the Slippery Slope: Ethics and Public Policy', *Kennedy Institute of Ethics Journal* 4 (1994), 209–25

Meilaender, Gilbert, 'Begetting and Cloning', in Gregory Pence (ed.), *Flesh of my Flesh: The Ethics of Cloning Humans* (Lanham, MD: Rowman & Littlefield, 1998), 39–44

Midgley, Mary, 'Biotechnology and Monstrosity', *Hastings Center Report* 30.5 (2000), 7–15

Mitchell, C. Ben, 'Genetic Renaissance in a Moral Dark Age', *Commentary provided by The Center for Bioethics and Human Dignity,* http://www.bioethix.org, 26 June 2000

—, 'Beyond the Impasse to What?', *Christianity Today,* 21 August 2000

Monod, Jacques, *Chance and Necessity* (English edn., Glasgow: Collins, 1972)

National Advisory Board on Ethics in Reproduction, 'Report on Human Cloning through Embryo Splitting: An Amber Light', *Kennedy Institute of Ethics Journal* 4 (1994), 251–82

National Bioethics Advisory Commission, 'Report on Cloning by the US Bioethics Advisory Commission: Ethical Considerations', *Human Reproduction Update* 3 (1997), 629–41

—, *Ethical Issues in Human Stem Cell Research* (Rockville, MD: National Bioethics Advisory Commission, 1999)

Nazir-Ali, Michael, 'A growing concern for us all', *Third Way,* October 2000, 4

Nuffield Council on Bioethics, *Stem Cell Therapy: The Ethical Issues* (London: Nuffield Council on Bioethics, 2000)

Peters, Ted, 'Cloning Shock: A Theological Reaction' in Ronald Cole-Turner (ed.), *Human Cloning: Religious Responses* (Louisville, KY: Westminster / John Knox Press 1997), 12–24

Polkinghorne Committee, *Review of the Guidance on the Research Use of Fetuses and Fetal Material* (London: HMSO, 1989)

Polkinghorne, John, *Beyond Science* (Cambridge: Cambridge University Press, 1996)

President's Commission for the Study of Ethical Problems in Medicine and Biomedical and Behavioral Research, *Splicing Life: The Social and Ethical Issues of Genetic Engineering with Human Beings* (Washington, DC: US Government Printing Office, 1982)

Ramsey, Paul, *Fabricated Man: The Ethics of Genetic Control* (New Haven: Yale University Press, 1970)

Reichenbach, Bruce R., and V. Elving Anderson, *On Behalf of God* (Grand Rapids, MI: Eerdmans, 1995)

Reubinoff, B.E., et al., 'Embryonic Stem Cell Lines from Human Blastocysts: Somatic Differentiation *In Vitro*', *Nature Biotechnology* 18 (2000), 399–404

Rorvik, David, *In His Image* (Melbourne: Thomas Nelson, 1978)

Sagan, Carl, *The Dragons of Eden* (New York: Random House, 1977)

—, *Cosmos* (New York: Random House, 1980)

Schlaudraff, Udo, 'How to Become an Ethicist? A Narrative Reflection', *Bulletin of Medical Ethics* (April 2000), 13–20

Shamblott, M.J., et al., 'Derivation of Pluripotent Stem Cells from Cultured Human Primordial Germ Cells', *Proceedings of the National Academy of Sciences USA* 95 (1998), 13726–31

Snowden, R., et al., *Artificial Reproduction: A Social Investigation* (London: George Allen & Unwin, 1983)

Thomson, J.A., et al., 'Embryonic Stem Cell Lines derived from Human Blastocysts', *Science* 282 (1998), 1145–7

Verhey, Allen D., 'Cloning: Revisiting an Old Debate, *Kennedy Institute of Ethics Journal* 4 (1994), 227–34

Willadsen, S.M., 'Nuclear Transfer in Sheep Embryos', *Nature* 320 (1986), 63–5

Wilmut, I., et al., *The Second Creation* (London: Headline, 2000)

—, 'Viable Offspring Derived from Fetal and Adult Mammalian Cells', *Nature* 385 (1997), 10–13

Index of Names

Subject Index